WAY TO INNER PEACE

Way to Inner Peace

FULTON J. SHEEN

ALBA · HOUSE   NEW · YORK

SOCIETY OF ST. PAUL, 2187 VICTORY BLVD., STATEN ISLAND, NEW YORK 10314

ST PAULS

Library of Congress Cataloging-in-Publication Data

Sheen, Fulton J. (Fulton John), 1895-1979.
    Way to inner peace / Fulton J. Sheen.
        p.   cm.
    Originally published: Garden City, N.Y.: Garden City Books, 1955.
    ISBN 0-8189-09713-4
    1. Christian life — Catholic authors.   2. Peace of mind — Religious
aspects — Catholic Church.   I. Title.
    BX2350.S54   1995
    248.4'82 — dc20   94-41422
                                                   CIP

Nihil Obstat:
John M.A. Fearns, STD
Censor Librorum

Imprimatur:
Francis Cardinal Spellman
Archbishop of New York
New York: January 26, 1955

The Nihil Obstat and Imprimatur are official declarations
that a book or pamphlet is free of doctrinal or moral
error. No implication is contained therein that those
who have granted the Nihil Obstat and Imprimatur agree
with the contents, opinions or statements expressed.

Produced and designed in the United States of America by the
Fathers and Brothers of the Society of St. Paul,
2187 Victory Boulevard, Staten Island, New York 10314,
as part of their communications apostolate.

ISBN: 0-8189-0713-4

Printing Information:

Current Printing - first digit	4	5	6	7	8	9	10

Year of Current Printing - first year shown

	2000	2001	2002	2003

Table of Contents

External Influences

Virtue

Learning

Wisdom

Table of Contents

Biblical Abbreviations

OLD TESTAMENT

Genesis	Gn	Nehemiah	Ne	Baruch	Ba
Exodus	Ex	Tobit	Tb	Ezekiel	Ezk
Leviticus	Lv	Judith	Jdt	Daniel	Dn
Numbers	Nb	Esther	Est	Hosea	Ho
Deuteronomy	Dt	1 Maccabees	1 M	Joel	Jl
Joshua	Jos	2 Maccabees	2 M	Amos	Am
Judges	Jg	Job	Jb	Obadiah	Ob
Ruth	Rt	Psalms	Ps	Jonah	Jon
1 Samuel	1 S	Proverbs	Pr	Micah	Mi
2 Samuel	2 S	Ecclesiastes	Ec	Nahum	Na
1 Kings	1 K	Song of Songs	Sg	Habakkuk	Hab
2 Kings	2 K	Wisdom	Ws	Zephaniah	Zp
1 Chronicles	1 Ch	Sirach	Si	Haggai	Hg
2 Chronicles	2 Ch	Isaiah	Is	Malachi	Ml
Ezra	Ezr	Jeremiah	Jr	Zechariah	Zc
		Lamentations	Lm		

NEW TESTAMENT

Matthew	Mt	Ephesians	Ep	Hebrews	Heb
Mark	Mk	Philippians	Ph	James	Jm
Luke	Lk	Colossians	Col	1 Peter	1 P
John	Jn	1 Thessalonians	1 Th	2 Peter	2 P
Acts	Ac	2 Thessalonians	2 Th	1 John	1 Jn
Romans	Rm	1 Timothy	1 Tm	2 John	2 Jn
1 Corinthians	1 Cor	2 Timothy	2 Tm	3 John	3 Jn
2 Corinthians	2 Cor	Titus	Tt	Jude	Jude
Galatians	Gal	Philemon	Phm	Revelation	Rv

WAY TO INNER PEACE

INNER PEACE

1. Egotism — the Enemy of Inner Peace

Here is a psychological suggestion for acquiring peace of soul. Never brag; never talk about yourself; never rush to first seats at table or in a theater; never use people for your own advantage; never lord it over others as if you were better than they.

These are but popular ways of expressing the virtue of humility, which does not consist so much in humbling ourselves before others as it does in recognizing our own littleness in comparison to what we ought to be. The modern tendency is toward the affirmation of the ego, the exaltation of selfishness, riding roughshod over others in order to satisfy our own self-centeredness. It certainly has not produced much happiness, for the more the ego asserts itself the more miserable it becomes.

Humility which gives preference to others is not very popular today, principally because men have forgotten the Greatness of God. By expanding our puny little self to the infinite, we have made the true Infinity of God seem trivial. The less knowledge we have of anything the more insignificant it seems. Our hatred of a person often decreases as we learn to know him better. A boy graduating from high school is generally not as humble as when he graduates from medical school. At eighteen he thought he knew it all; at twenty-eight he feels himself ignorant in the face of the medical science he has yet to acquire. So it is with God. Because we do not pray or contemplate or love Him, we become vain and proud; but when we know Him better we feel a deep sense of dependence which tempers our false independence. Pride is the child of ignorance, humility the offspring of knowledge.

Proud people think themselves to be better than they are, and when criticized always believe their neighbor is jealous or has a grudge against them. The humble know themselves as they really are, for they judge themselves as they judge time, by a standard outside themselves, namely, God and His Moral Law. The psychological reason for the modern fondness for news which deflates others or brings out the evil in their lives, is to solace uneasy consciences which are already laden with guilt. By finding others who apparently are more evil than we, we falsely believe that we are somehow better "than the rest of men" (Lk 18:11). It used to be that the most popular biographies were stories about the lives of good men and women worthy of our imitation, rather than the recounting of scandals for the sake of making us believe we are more virtuous than we really are. The pagan Plutarch said: "The virtues of great men served me as a modern mirror in which I might adorn my own life."

Humility as it relates to others is a golden mean between blind reverence on the one hand and an overbearing insolence on the other. Humble people are not rigid exacters of things to which they have no undoubted right; they are always ready to overlook the faults of others knowing that they have so many themselves. Neither are they greatly provoked at those slights which put vain persons out of patience, knowing that as we show mercy to others so shall we receive mercy from God. Before undertaking a task great or small, before making decisions, before beginning a journey, the humble will acknowledge their dependence on God and will invoke His guidance and His blessing on all their enterprises. Even though they be placed above others by vocation, or by the will of the people, they will never cease to recognize that God has made of one blood all the nations that dwell on the earth. If they are very rich they will not be "defenders of the rights of the poor" without unloading their riches in their aid. Our modern world has produced a generation of rich politicians who talk love of the poor, but never prove it in action, and a brood of the poor whose hearts are filled with envy for the rich and covetousness of their money. The rich who are humble help rather than use the poor to pave their way to power.

Another evidence of want of humility is in regard to knowledge. Scripture bids us to be wise and "correctly interpret the word of truth" (2 Tm 2:15). Humility moderates our estimate of what we know and will remind us that God gave to the wise more talents than others and more opportunities for developing those talents. But of him who has received much, much also will be expected. The intellectual leader has a tremendous responsibility thrust upon him and woe to him if he uses his office of teaching to lead the young into error and conceit. Notice how often today authors will have their picture taken with their book in their left hand, the title in full view of the camera, so that the photograph may tell the story: "Look Ma! My Book!" Television commentators have books on their desks with the title toward the audience so that the audience may be impressed. No one who reads books at a desk ever has the titles turned away — but toward himself. Perhaps some day when there are diaphanous walls, the intelligentsia will keep the titles on their bookshelves turned toward the wall so their next door neighbor will know how smart they are.

In the face of Divine Wisdom, all that we have, or do, or know, is a gift of God, and is only an insignificant molehill compared to His Mountain of Knowledge. Well indeed then may those who enjoy any relative superiority ask with Paul: "What do you have that you haven't received? And if you've received it, why do you boast as if it were yours alone?" (1 Cor 4:7).

2. *Trials of Our Own Making*

An educator was once asked by a mother of a child of five years of age, at what age she should begin educating her child. His answer was that "it is already five years too late." This may be an exaggeration, but the best informed opinions are that the two ages which are most important in the education of the young are the ages between three and four for psychological development, and the beginning of the "teens" for ethical development.

The age of three or four is important because at this age self-consciousness begins; the child makes a clear distinction between itself and its environment, between his actions and the reactions it receives from the outside world. It is also the age when the child sees itself, looks at itself as in a mirror, reflects, and comes to some conclusion as to whether the world is easy or hard.

Many parents today are encouraging their children to believe that they are the "smartest kids in schools"; that nothing they do is wrong; that if they had the opportunity to be on television like some of those other "lucky kids," they would be a thousand times better. The result is that when they grow up they are full of false fantasies about their presumed superiority. If they do not succeed in business, later on, it is because someone was "prejudiced" or "jealous" of them; if they become painters and anyone criticizes their work, they go into a rage; their best friends are those who tolerate them, while they have nothing but disdain for those who do not flatter and praise them. Their fantasy is taken for reality; the false for the true.

Those who are pampered during youth thus retain a delusion of grandeur during life and are very subject to physical and mental breakdowns. The breakdown is psychologically induced, though they are very unconscious of it. The breakdown is for the sake of the preservation of the fantasy. Some will develop muscular pains and sickness in order to avoid the test of their greatness. Then they can say, "If it were not for being bedridden, I would have written the best novel of the day." The bubble of his fantasy would be pricked, if he had to abandon the pretense of being so great. So he stays sick to prevent the test.

From the spiritual point of view, the basic trouble with such people is pride, egotism or selfishness. Their complexes are due to a great extent to a want of practice of the virtue of humility. They have developed the wrong treasures, and therefore the heart is in the wrong place. As Our Blessed Lord said, "For where your treasure is, there will your heart be also" (Mt 6:21; Lk 12:34). It makes little difference whether we possess the treasure or not; what matters is that we love it. In this case, the treasure is the exalted opinion we have of self, or having our own will satisfied. If this be the treasure, then all the affections, desires and feelings we have intertwine about our ego. Our real good is that which we work most earnestly to preserve, and which saddens us most when we lose it. Hence the frequency with which we praise ourselves because of the money we made, or the oil wells we dug. As the sunflower turns toward the sun, the magnetic needle to the polestar, so the egotist turns to his fantasy.

Such persons are really still infants, for the characteristic note of an infant is that it wants everything it sees and it cries when it does not get it. By constantly seeking pleasure of self, the tone has been ruined. So many of our cares today are of our own making. Never before were there so many woes manufactured by our own hands. "Made by me and made within" could be stamped on most of the trials and difficulties that people endure. God gives us the strength to bear the sorrows of our own. Those who make their own trials are also those who never call upon Him for aid; those who have sorrows laid on them by God always do. The serpents that sting us are from within and not without, we carry them in our own bosom — this is the tragedy. When the earthy treasures are swept away, those who trust in God have everything left.

3. *Faithfulness in Little Things*

Faithfulness in great things is not uncommon; faithfulness in little things is rare but most indicative of true character. Almost any husband would leap into the sea or rush into a burning building to rescue his perishing wife. But to anticipate the convenience or happiness of the wife in some small matter, the neglect of which would go unnoticed, is a more eloquent proof of tenderness.

Our lives for the most part are made up of little things, and by these our character is to be tested. There are very few who have to take a prominent place in the great conflicts of our age; the vast majority must dwell in humbler scenes and be content to do a more humble work. The conflicts which we have to endure either against evil in our own soul or in the moral circle where our influence would seem to be trivial are in reality the struggle of the battle for life and decency; and true heroism is shown here as well as in those grander scales in which others win the leader's fame or the martyr's crown. Little duties carefully discharged; little temptations earnestly resisted with the strength which God supplies; little sins crucified; these all together help to form that character which is to be described not as popular or glamorous, but as moral and noble.

From God's point of view nothing is great, nothing is small as we measure it. The worth and the quality of any action depends upon its motive and not at all upon its prominence or any of the other accidents which we are apt to adopt as standards of greatness. Nothing is small that can be done from a mighty motive, such as the mite which the widow dropped into the Temple treasury. Conscience knows no such word as "large" or "small"; it knows only two words, "right" and "wrong." "He who welcomes a prophet because he is a prophet shall receive the reward given to prophets," because though not gifted with the prophet's tongue he has the prophet's spirit and does his small act of hospitality from the very same prophetic impulse which in another and one more loftily endowed leads to burning words and mighty deeds.

A man is much more inclined to concentrate his moral actions in one great moment and thereby often wins the merit of a hero. A woman, on the contrary, scatters her tiny little sacrifices through life and multiplies them to such an extent that very few give her the credit for sacrifice because it has been so multiplied.

In the spiritual order it is much easier to do some mighty act of self-surrender than daily and patiently to crucify the flesh with all of its inordinate affections. The smallest duties are often harder, because of their apparent insignificance and their constant recurrence. Unfaithfulness in little things can also prepare for unfaithfulness in the great. By a small act of injustice the line which separates the right from the wrong is just as effectively broken. Infidelity in little things deteriorates the moral sense; it makes a person untrustworthy; it loosens the ties that bind society together, and it is a counteracting agency of that Divine Love which ought to be the cement of good human relationships.

Men in public life who are accused of confiscating great sums of money or else profiting by their office to secure gifts or enrich themselves in any manner whatsoever, began with unfaithfulness in the minor details of life. Somewhere and somehow the wall and partition between right and wrong had to be broken down, and what is tragic about our national situation is that there is no longer a moral indignation against such infractions of the law of honesty.

Little things make up the universe. The clouds gather up the rain and moisture and part with them in drops; time is so precious that it is given out second by second; stars do not leap about in their orbits but keep a measured pace. In like manner, humans will find little to do if they save their energy for great occasions. In every direction the great is reached through the little. The turning of a tiny needle steadily toward a fixed point is a little common thing, but it guides navies along the uncharted seas. The most significant trifle becomes a great thing if the alternative of obedience or rebellion is involved in it. To live by the day and to watch each step is the true pilgrimage method, for there is nothing little if God requires it.

4. Knowledge but No Truth

Never before in the history of the world was there so much wealth, and never before so much poverty; never before was there so much power, and never before so little peace; never before so much education, and never before so little coming to the knowledge of the truth. This latter discrepancy is the Scriptural sign of "perilous times."

This does not mean that our generation is not studious, nor an uninterested inquirer, nor wanting in a thirst for knowledge. As a matter of fact, there is not a university professor in the country who does not use many times in the course of the year, the hackneyed phrase that he is interested in "extending the horizons of knowledge." We are all bent on attaining the new, but not succinctly concerned with utilizing what we already possess. Everyone boasts that he loves to knock at the door of truth, but the sad fact is that if the door opened, many would die of the shock. They much prefer to hear the sound of their knuckles on the portals, rather than to accept responsibilities which truth implies. We do not even want to hear truth about ourselves.

Knowing many things is different from knowing truth, just as a crazy quilt is different from a blueprint. Ten thousand isolated bits of knowledge do not make for understanding, any more than the mixture of all the bottles on the shelves of a druggist makes for health. A corpse has chemical elements as well as a live body, but a corpse lacks unity which only the soul can supply. What the soul is to the body, that truth is to knowledge; what the architect and his plan are to a building, that truth is to an education.

One of the most dangerous effects of reducing education to the amassing of knowledge rather than the acquisition of truth, is that it forgets the relationship between truth and character. If a person does not know the true purpose of an explosive, he may hurt himself. The same effects do not follow from one point of view about the contents of a bottle as from another. If the bottle is filled with poison, it will do little good to the one who takes it to maintain that he was sincere in his belief that it contained bourbon. A boxer can be very "sincere" about his belief that he ought always to lead with his right, but all may not be right in the end. A farmer may be sincere in planting thistles, but he will not raise corn.

- 14 -

On the other hand, because people know the truth, their conduct will not necessarily be good. But at any rate, they had a map: they know where they ought to go. If they get off the road they will not blame their ductless glands or their grandmother. Even though they are off the road, they know there is a right road. The tragedy of today is that the world is not only tearing up the photographs of a good society, but also tearing up the negatives. By denying truth the world gives up the search for it, just as the person who believes that blindness is normal will never seek a cure.

It does not make a whale of a difference what people believe about party politics, for parties in a democracy generally represent indifferently good means to a good end, namely the preservation of the common good. It makes little difference in the moral character of a person whether we believe golf is better exercise than tennis, but it makes all the difference in the world whether we believe that a human being is a creature of God or a beast. It may take a few years for such wrong philosophy to work itself out in action, just as it takes time for cockle sown instead of wheat to appear in the harvest field, but eventually it does appear. If we are wrong in the purpose of life, we are wrong on everything. The soul is dyed with the color of its beliefs. A popular bromide is to say: "If I do my best, it will be all right." The Income Tax Bureau will not accept that philosophy. To "have done our best" will not console us much if we still miss a train or fail a bar examination. The road to hell is paved with good intentions.

Education is presently directed to help students answer the question: "What can I do?" If a pencil were endowed with consciousness, it would not first ask itself: "What can I do?" but rather: "What am I?" "What is my purpose?" Once that was established, then the pencil would be prepared for writing. When our youth has discovered the Truth about life, two conclusions will follow: courage to be oneself, and humility to recognize our creatureliness; that being a product, a result, a creature of the Power that made us, we will seek with the help of that Power to be all that we can be — a human being worthy of the name — aye, more than a human being — a child of God!

5. No Truth without Humility

Whenever a new scientific theory is born there are not wanting intelligentsia who set it to music so that every other kind of knowledge in the world dances to its tunes. When Comte developed sociology, then everything was socialized, even God; when Darwin developed evolution, then everything was evolutionized, including morals; now that relativity has been established, non-scientists make everything relative, saying there is no such thing as Truth or Goodness — these are relative to your point of view. Quite apart from the fact that the theory of relativity does not deny an absolute for it is based on the absoluteness of the spread of light — it is rather absurd to apply the methods of one branch of knowledge to all other branches of knowledge. Relativity, for example, does not mean that we have six toes on one foot counted one way, and four toes on the other foot counted another way.

The denial of Truth is just as fatal to the mind as the denial of light is to vision. Truth in its fullness is not easy to attain, even if one does admit its existence. There are certain psychological and spiritual conditions which are essential for its discovery, and the most important of these is the virtue of humility.

Humility is not a want of moral force; rather humility is a recognition of the truth about ourselves. To explore the Truth in all its complexity there must come moments when we confess ignorance, when we frankly admit that we were mistaken or bigoted, or prejudiced. These admissions are painful, but they actually enrich character just as much as all approximations to falsehood forfeit it. If we are proud, covetous, conceited, selfish, lustful, constantly wanting our own way, it is far better to come face to face with our own ugliness than to live in a fool's paradise. The basis of all criticism of neighbor, the source of false judgments, slander, jealousies and pulling down the reputation of others is our refusal to look into our own soul. Since the sense of justice in us is so deep and ineradicable, if we do not make ourselves just by conforming to truth, we find fault with others in the vain hope of establishing justice in them. We are all stronger for knowing the worst we can about ourselves and then acting on that knowledge. When we explain away our conceits by psychological jargon we increase our inner mental discomfort, as the denial of a physical illness gives random speed to the disease.

The growth of democracy has done much to do away with a false social snobbishness and to keep men humble in their external relations. But it has also, from another point of view, weakened the respect for Goodness and Truth, inasmuch as the masses of people are generally inclined to equate morality with the general level of society at any given moment. Numbers become the measure of goodness. If a sufficient number can be counted who violate a certain Commandment of God, then it is argued: "Fifty million adulterers cannot be wrong. We have to change the Commandments." The excellence of moral excellence does not reside in any external conformity to a conventional standard, but in an inward disposition under the control of a recognized principle to which we submit whether we agree with it or not.

Humility is required to challenge mediocrity; one must be ready to brave the taunts of those who knock anyone in the head who raises himself above the level of the masses. Mediocrity can be a terrific form of tyranny, and it has a thousand and one penalties for those who forsake the external standards for an inward change of heart to a line of conduct above the level. When a thousand people are walking to the edge of an abyss, the one who is seen walking in the opposite direction is taunted for not following the mob. We must be humble to bear up under these reproaches and dare to be right when the majority is wrong.

Thus humility is the pathway to Truth and inner peace is grounded on the recognition of two dimensions beyond the flatness of the mass level: one is the recognition of the dimension of height, which is the Sanctity above, the other is the dimension of depth, which is the existence of evil within the human heart.

6. Desire

Desire is to the soul what gravitation is to matter. When we know our desires, we know the direction our soul is taking. If desire is heavenly, we go upwards, if it is wholly earthly, we go downwards. Desire is like raw material out of which we fashion either our virtues or vices. As Our Lord said: "Where your treasure is, there your heart is also."

Very few people ever withdraw enough from the world to ask themselves what is their basic desire. There are some who live a seemingly good life, who pay taxes, contribute to advertised welfare needs, but their basic desires are evil. Their goodness is often a want of opportunity for doing what is sinful. They are like the Elder Son in the Parable of the Prodigal Son who accuses his brother of "wasting his substance on harlots." There was nothing of this kind in the story. But the accusation revealed that the Elder Son would have done this very thing if he had been his brother.

On the other hand, there are some people who do very evil things, but who have a basic desire to be good, and are waiting for the day when a helpful hand will lift them from the pit. It was of such a group that Our Lord said: "Tax collectors and prostitutes are entering the Kingdom of God ahead of you [Scribes and Pharisees]" (Mt 21:31).

Contentment depends upon the control of our desires. Advertising serves many needs but it has also made luxuries appear as necessities, and created a desire for goods which the individual cannot possibly possess in their fullness. The Eastern World has struck on the secret of inner peace by suggesting that inner happiness is dependent on the control and limitation of desires. St. Paul said: "I have learned to be content with what I have" (Ph 4:11). Contentment is not indifference though the ignorant sometimes make that identification. Contentment does not mean immunity from trial, for it can know sighs and tears, but its feelings are never allowed to run into fretfulness. If it can not have what it wants, it never broods over its disappointments but brightens them by sweet submission. It has no kinship with fatalism which refuses to plan or act in the belief that nothing can be altered. It is such fatalism which characterizes certain Eastern philosophies and makes progress impossible. In contentment one does not submit before he has prayed and acted, but after one has done all he can, accepting the event as the will of the Lord.

There is a world of difference between submitting to the Divine Will from sullenness and submitting to it knowing that God is Supreme Wisdom, and that some day we will know all that happened, happened for the best. There is a marvelous peace that comes into the soul if all trials and disappointments, sorrows and pains are accepted either as a deserved chastisement for our sins, or as a healthful discipline which will lead us to greater virtue. The violin strings, if they were conscious, would complain when the musician tightened them, but this is because they do not see that the sacrificial strain was necessary before they could produce a perfect melody. Evils actually become lighter by patient endurance and benefits are poisoned by discontent.

Contentment is based on the idea that "our sufficiency is not from ourselves but from God." The soul does not desire or lack more than what God has supplied him. His will suits his state after he has exhausted his resources and his desire does not exceed his power. Hence everything that happens is judged to be as good and worthy of Divine appointment. As Socrates observed: "He is nearest to God who needs the fewest things."

Contentment is not inconsistent with our endeavor to have our condition improved. We do everything we can, as if all depended on us, but we trust in God as if everything depended on Him. The talents we have must be put to work, but if they yield only a certain return, we do not murmur because the return is not greater. When we really examine our consciences we have to admit that we have received more than we morally deserved! The discontent is far greater among the over-privileged than the underprivileged. The rich need the psychoanalysts more than the poor. Few European minds cracked under two wars. Many American minds have. The first learned not to expect anything. This lesson America has yet to learn.

GOODNESS

7. Goodness Needs Publicity

An organ can produce a thunderous outburst of discordant sounds but it can also, when played properly, give forth the most soothing and peaceful melodies. So it is with human passions. They can be used without regard to law or they can be governed to foster joy and affection.

A person may have the knowledge of music and yet not enjoy it, as Nietzsche did before his madness as he thumped the keys of the piano with his elbows. So too we may have a knowledge of love and yet not show love to others.

One wonders if an apology for want of love is not the effect of sampling one person out of every ten thousand and then writing a history of their passions. Would it not tend to substitute statistical average for a noble emotion? Then, too, is it scientific? Suppose we decided to write a history of the United States, and took only one day of every ten thousand days. That would be writing one event every twenty-seven years.

What one sets out to find, one generally finds. Those who are critical by nature, almost always find faults in others. If we start with the assumption that most people are dishonest, are we not constantly bumping up against crooks? On the contrary, if we believe people to be kind and good-hearted, these are about the only kind of souls we ever meet. They who are afraid of accidents most generally have them; their first principle of always looking for the worst makes the worst appear. Sometimes it is possible to tell a person to hide something in a room, and later discover the hiding place by taking hold of his hand and following its instinctive motions. When one begins with the idea that infidelity is common and that one ought to search for it, it is very likely that one will instinctively go to those areas and persons where infidelity is most likely to be found, and avoid those other groups or people where infidelity is less likely to be manifested. Tramps coming to New York, even for the first time, land in the Bowery, not on Park Avenue. What we *believe* is to a great extent a determinant of where we will go, like an alcoholic to a bar, and a Christian to a church.

The mood of our century is critical, partly because of its own uneasy conscience. "Misery loves company," it is said but so also does evil. The good has but few publicists. Most newspaper editors love murders, graft and scandals, but how few ever headline virtue. And yet the world is so full of good people, heroic deeds, generous hearts. Take the most sublime act of love that is possible in this world, namely dying as a martyr rather than deny the God of Love. Never in history have there been as many martyrs as there are today. The martyrdoms of the first 250 years of Christian history are trivial in comparison to the unnumbered heroes of the soul who have died for the faith today. This is loyalty! This is fidelity! And any civilizations that can produce martyrs on such a high level must necessarily produce them on a lower level even in the home. What heat is to the natural universe, that love is to the moral universe.

It is love that needs sampling today, mostly because love does so little advertising of its own. Being humble by nature, like the violet, it is served by few propagandists. Cities report births as well as deaths; why then should not publicists be as interested in those who love as well as those who betray? It is part of the perversity of human nature to give more space to an ancient or a modern Benedict Arnold who betrayed his country than to ten thousand patriots who died for it. But the solemn fact remains that faithfulness, honor, control of errant impulses and love keep the world at peace. It would be well for us, in these days when men look for evil and find it, to look for good and diffuse it — in particular among the millions of cases of disinterested love where others are served, with no hope of ever receiving even an empty hand in grateful clasp.

8. Perfection Is Not Automatic

Whenever anyone hears of a new psychological theory such as the ability to see the future in a dim way, or reads of a drug which retards old age, there is almost a cosmic rush to the conclusion that in a few years humanity will be free from error and immune from disease. This urge to perfection is right and good, for there is no reason why the evolutionary process should stand still once it comes to human beings.

But the fallacy is that we human beings always think of this perfection as coming to us without our own effort or the exercise of our own free will. Perfection is regarded as available without cost, but not like the crown of effort such as playing the piano, which is born of a thousand acts of the will and the tediousness of exercises. Perfection is thus taken out of the moral order and reduced to the physical order; it is something that is given to us, rather than something we acquire; it comes like a surprise legacy which we did not earn nor merit, rather than as a prize which was won by blood and sweat and tears. The truth is that perfection has something to do with becoming what we are not, and that this becoming is achieved through willing, self-discipline and even suffering, and implies an ideal above us and one toward which we strive.

Perfection is the plenitude of goodness, or the

uniting within ourselves of goodness and happiness. This in turn demands distinction and comparison. For example, suppose a person wished to be a good archaeologist, such as one of the greatest of them all, Heinrich Schliemann. Three factors were required: (1) A recognition of the fact that there was much to learn; (2) A realization of an ideal and the working toward it as the task of his life; (3) A sense of his own imperfection. This sense of imperfection came to him as a boy of seven, when his father told him about the heroes of Homer and how the mighty city of Troy was levelled and burned. The idea of perfection, from the point of view of Greek archaeology, would be to discover the city of Troy. When his father told him that nobody knew where the city of Troy stood, to him perfection was expressed in the sentence: "When I am big, I shall go to Greece and find Troy and the King's Treasure." The third stage was the development of that idea. He learned many modern languages, studied Greek history and Homer until he knew him by heart. Finally, in the year 1873, after digging up 325,000 cubic yards of earth, he found Troy and the King's Treasure.

But there is not only archaeological perfection, there is also human perfection, that is, our growth in goodness as human beings. This too implies three terms: The first two are correlative — a sense of our own imperfection and an idea of perfection which is God. The more we believe we know it all, and that we have never done anything wrong for which we have to expiate our guilt, the less is our impulse toward anything better. That is why subjectively, though not objectively, the more we inflate our ego the less important God seems to be. The sick person recognizes the need of a physician; the ignorant mind senses the need of a teacher; and the soul which recognizes its own unworthiness yearns for God to complete its personality.

In between these two correlatives, namely the thirst and the fountain, hunger and the Bread of Life, there comes the third essential for moral perfection, namely, an act of the will by which one begins to lop off imperfections through restraint, sacrifice, self-discipline, and begins the positive achievement toward the Divine goal. What impels us toward this perfection is love, for when we love perfection, we eliminate everything which offends the Loved One. For example, a girl will wear red, even though she does not like it, because she knows it pleases her beloved. Michelangelo once was asked how he carved his statues. He said that it was very easy. Inside of every block of marble is a beautiful form. All you have to do is cut away the marble and the form will appear. In like manner, in every person there is a possible new self, the Ideal self. All one has to do is first to have an image of the model before one and trust in His grace, and then cut off huge chunks of selfishness and egotism until the Divine Image appears.

9. Our Neighbors in Distress

In the parable of the Good Samaritan (Lk 10:30-37) it is said that a priest and a Levite passed by the wounded man and help was given him by one of another race — namely, the Samaritan. We do not know whatever happened to the priest and the Levite, but it is very likely that they went into Jerusalem and reported the condition of the dying man to a social service agency. The point of the parable is that some neighbors have to be helped in their emergency at the cost of our convenience. The neighbor is not the one who lives next door, nor the one with whom we have a nodding acquaintance. What makes someone a neighbor is love in the heart. When this is wanting it avails nothing that a person lives in the same block, or belongs to the same club, for none of these external bonds can supply the place of love.

No doubt those who saw the Samaritan aid the wounded traveler would have said that he was a neighbor or an old friend, but the truth of the matter is that the Samaritan did not know the wounded man at all — it was his genuine compassion and affection that made the Samaritan his brother and his neighbor and a friend.

The story of the Good Samaritan was told in answer to the question of a lawyer: "Who is my neighbor?" The answer of the parable is: "Every person in distress is your neighbor." Sometimes that neighbor is the one who is least capable of making known his condition. Not long ago one of the nationally known picture magazines had a photograph of a man prostrate on subway stairs. For thirty minutes many people passed him by without ever a helping hand. The editorial comment was about the coldness of the modern world in the face of distress. What was forgotten was that the photographer of the picture magazine did nothing for thirty minutes for the afflicted individual except to snap pictures and make his own living. The unfortunate traveler on the road between Jericho and Jerusalem could make no importunate supplications for relief, could not even ask for help. The need is often greatest where the least is asked. How many forms of misery are there lying within our knowledge as we journey through the bloodstained road of life. We pass them by because they do not bar our progress or because it is possible for us to put them out of our mind and live as if they were not in it.

The best way to help others is by identifying ourselves with their affliction, getting into them and feeling their pains as our own. It is not enough merely to have an intellectual understanding of another person's difficulty; we need to go a little farther to feel it as our own burden, as the Samaritan put the wounded man upon a beast of burden and took him to an inn. On the other hand, if we have a trial and want to get mastery over it, the best person to go to is the one who has gained a victory over the same temptation. If one has marital difficulties and is inclined to leave the spouse, the worst person to go to is a psychiatrist who is already divorced and remarried. The best one to convert a drunkard is a converted drunkard. Power to appreciate temptation is the fine condition of being able to help others out of temptation. The first step God took toward making us become like Him was to become, as far as He could, like us.

The powerful are always under obligation to the weak. Advantage of any kind is not a personal possession but a trust. St. Paul said: "I am obligated to both Greeks and barbarians; to the wise and the foolish alike" (Rm 1:14). In reality, of course, he owed the Greeks nothing — they had persecuted him; and the barbarians he had never seen. But Paul was conscious that God had conferred upon him great gifts and he felt bound to share these gifts with others who did not yet possess them.

It is such willing generosity that marks the true lover of humankind. There are two kinds of liquors and juices, those that pour themselves out and drop of their own accord, and those that have to be squeezed and pressed out by violence. The latter give but grudgingly; the former are generally found more sweet. Those who help others reluctantly are like the reluctant juices. It is a long time before the purse can be found and before the hand can get in it to find change; when they give they do it in such a manner as if to indicate that the hand had stolen from the heart unaware and that the eye was displeased with the discovery of the theft.

Love that desires to limit its own exercise is not love. Love that is happier if it meets only one who needs help than if it met ten, and happiest if it met none at all, is not love. One of love's essential laws is expressed in the words of Our Lord that the Apostles fondly remembered after He ascended: "It is more blessed to give than to receive" (Ac 20:35). Our nation will be happier and our hearts will be more full of joy when we discover the true brotherhood of man, but to do this we must realize that we are a race of illegitimate children unless there is also the Fatherhood of God.

10. The So-Called "Good" People

A little girl once prayed that God would make all the "bad" people good, and all the "good" people nice. By the "good" people she meant those who were narrow in their goodness, therefore, those who were not fundamentally good. It is a spiritual and a psychological fact that some people who pride themselves on their virtue resent sinners mending their ways. This was the position of the elder son in the parable of the Prodigal Son, who complained that the father had welcomed home his younger brother with a feast. As it turns out, the parable is the story of two sons who deserved to lose their father's love (although neither one actually did because the father was so kind) — one because he was too "bad," the other because he was too "good."

Jealousy or the grudging of good to others causes many minds to rejoice in the failures and sufferings of others. Secretly they feel that sin in others pulls them down to their level, or at least the others no longer enjoy superiority. The fondness of the twentieth century for scandal is due to a great extent to its guilty conscience. By finding others' skirts stained with mud, some rejoice that their dusty and ragged ones are not so bad after all. The elder son complained to the father that he had obeyed him but received no reward. His good conduct evidently was not born of honest affections, but rather of self-interest. If he were interested in goodness, he would have rejoiced in the reformation of his brother. He seems even to regret that he had not wallowed in the same excesses of his brother — at least he thought they were excesses. There is no hint in the story that the prodigal son had ever read a Sex Report and decided to explore its depths with abandon. It is the elder son who introduces that note in the story. His own mind, therefore, was not strange to evil desires.

He could not understand the father's joy in seeing the younger son restored again to grace and virtue. How could this be, if it were not that in being virtuous, he had failed to see it as an ideal. Rather did he think that the removal of the younger brother's guilt deprived him of something that was his own.

The father tried to get his "good" son to understand that "all that I have is yours." He was saying: "You have never regarded your father as a father, but as a taskmaster." There are those who think of religion as made up of laws and commandments, and these never enter into the joy of sonship with the Heavenly Father. Some who remain in the father's house can be just as little a true son, as the son who became a voluntary outcast. The elder son was being told that he would enter into the father's blessedness when he would own his outcast member as a brother. This at first the elder son refused to do, even calling his brother "your son." If Christian people want feasts as their wages for virtue, it will not be God who pays them, but the devil. The reward is entering into the full possession of the Father's inheritance, so that the electricity of love passes even to those who once repudiated that love. Sons are tempted to say in their constant dedication to duty: "Have I kept my hands clean and have I

cleansed my heart in vain?" But it is not servile at-
tentiveness to duty that wins God's love; the father
had to convince the elder son that he loses nothing
by a gain in family relationship. No outward display
of confidence and affection is necessary because the
elder sons are with the father always. Love in such
a case must be taken for granted. Praise is given to
strangers frequently, but less to those of our own
household. Hence the father said it was fitting that
the elder son rejoice, because elder sons must learn
that sinners can be pardoned without withdrawing
a father's favors.

The lesson is not to be forgotten: in a not too
distant day when Russia, like the prodigal son, will
return to the father's house, let not Western civilization refuse to accept it back or absent itself from the
feast celebrating the salvation of what was lost. Constant obedience is better than repentance, but the
truly obedient will always rejoice in the repentant.

11. Restoring Stolen Goods

The most interesting tax collector in the history of
the world was Zacchaeus (Lk 19:1-10) — if you can
call any tax collector "interesting." Physically, he was
so short that whenever there was a parade, he al-

ways had to climb a tree in order to see it. His name meant "pure," but he was anything but that, for he was a "twenty-five per center," always taking that much at least out of what he collected for his "cut." But the end of the story reveals that he was much better than his neighbors believed him to be.

This particular day Our Blessed Lord came to the village, and Zacchaeus, as was his wont, climbed a sycamore tree. People that want for size must make up for it by sagacity. Not many tax collectors in our days, particularly those who are "rich," as was Zacchaeus, would humble themselves by elevating themselves in a tree. But Zacchaeus was rewarded, for Our Lord saw him and He asked him to take Him home. Whenever the Lord wants to give a favor, He often asks for one.

When the door was closed behind the two of them, the mob outside was angry, not with the tax collector because he was dishonest, but they were angry with Our Divine Lord because He ate with disreputable people and sinners. The Savior's way of looking at it was that He had found one sheep that went astray. After a few minutes the conscience of the tax collector was aroused — for consciences only sleep, they never die. Zacchaeus promised to make amends for his dishonesty by giving half of his goods to the poor and restoring fourfold to anyone whom he had cheated.

Restitution is a duty which a civilization that

stresses profits and money can readily forget. When anyone has been cheated, when capitalists under-pay their workers, when labor leaders during a strike destroy company property, when repairmen pile up needless expenses by the substitution of one item for another of less worth, when an honest day's work is not given for an honest day's pay, there is no dis-tribution of that equilibrium and balance of justice which makes the world livable. Remorse is not enough; shame is not enough; the balming of dis-honesty by saying one has an Oedipus complex or that one feared his grandmother are not enough; there must be a restoring of the property that was stolen. If the person who was cheated cannot be found, there must be a donation of an equal amount to the poor. Restitution is the restoring of a person to that condition from which, contrary to right and duty, we have removed him.

The reason for rendering satisfaction for our dishonesty is clear. The law of nature and the law of the land affirm that every one ought to possess in undisturbed use those goods to which he or she has a right. If we steal something from our neigh-bor at nine o'clock at night, it does not rightfully become ours at ten o'clock. In other words, the pass-ing of time does not change the right, nor make law-ful that which was illegal. Under the Levitical Law, the Jews were obliged to give "five oxen for an ox, and four sheep for a sheep." Time never cancels out the duty of restoring that which we have unjustly taken from another, regardless of how much sorrow we may have had for the theft. The proof that we are sorry is that we do return the stolen goods.

To make money dishonestly and then put it in the wife's name is not to escape the obligation to make restitution. Since such a person never owned the property lawfully, he never could make the transfer legally. Suppose a woman is sold a handkerchief on the pretence that it is silk, when really it is nylon — restitution must be made. A second-hand car dealer who tells a buyer that the car is in perfect condition, and yet knows that he filled the rear transmission with sawdust to hide for a hundred miles the defective gears — such a crook is certainly bound to make restitution.

There is a story — and it is only a story — about a man who went to confession to a priest. During confession he stole the priest's watch. He then told the priest that he had stolen a watch. The priest said: "You must make restitution." The thief said: "I'll give it to you, Father." "No," said the priest, "give it to the owner." The penitent said, "The owner won't take it back." "In that case," said the priest, "you can keep it."

If this were not a story, the penitent would still be bound to make restitution — not only to the priest from whom he had stolen the watch but also to God. Honesty is not a policy; it is a duty!

12. Hospitality

Great virtues are apt to pass out of civilization because the structure of society changes. When there were few cities and journeys were long and arduous, hospitality was one of the most frequently practiced virtues. Herodotus the Greek historian, tells us of being shipwrecked on a sparsely settled shore, and how a whole family went without food to care for him. One of our missionaries in the Pacific stated that he would never tell the natives of the island that he had even so much as a headache; otherwise they would sit up outside his tent the whole night boiling water and herbs, and holding themselves at attention in case of need.

Hospitality has not passed out of the world today, but to a large extent it has become corporate or organized. Institutions are set up to care for the traveler or the needy, as the care becomes less personal and the responsibility less individual. A few decades ago no one in a horse and buggy along a country road would refuse to stop and pick up someone walking. Today few automobiles stop to give lifts to those on the highway, mostly because too many hitchhikers have made hospitality impossible by their inhospitable conduct. Despite this, it is wrong to think the world is not fit to be trusted and that everyone is a rogue until he proves himself to be otherwise.

Granted the changing ways, the necessity of the virtue of hospitality still remains. Nor is it satisfied by identifying hospitality with the offer of a highball. The essence of hospitality is sympathy and kindness; it is selfishness which makes us think that the opportunities for hospitality are past.

> I thought the house across the way
> Was empty; but since yesterday
> Crepe on the door makes me aware
> That someone has been living there.

The age of discovery is not yet over and the greatest discovery yet remains to be made by every individual, namely, there are other people in the world besides oneself. As a former Prince of Wales once said: "Number Ten Downing Street can never be a substitute for the good neighbor"; neither can the Community Chest nor the Social Welfare Agency. Immediate personal contact, courageous embracing of the worries and burdens involved in full personal and intimate relationships — these are the bloodstream of a healthy society.

On the Last Day, Our Blessed Lord said that He will judge us by our attitude to hospitality: "When did we see you hungry or thirsty or a stranger or naked or sick or in prison and not care for you?" (Mt 25:44). Hospitality, therefore, not only has the duties of which we are aware, but also the more ter-

- 42 -

rible awareness that it is Christ Who is the Stranger. In all our dealings, we are dealing with the Lord Himself, though we know it not. Maybe if we could see our wars aright, in between two trenches of the enemies, or between a plane in the sky and the target beneath, there is Christ's Body being shot full of holes. What men do to one another, they do to Him, whether the act be of kindness or bitterness — and out of those acts will come our judgment.

The bold knight of the Round Table traveled far over mountain and desert in search of the Holy Grail, the Cup of Life from which the Savior drank the night of the Last Supper. His journeys proved fruitless. Depressed in spirit and fatigued in body, he returned to Arthur's hall. On the way he saw a poor man writhing in the ditch. Moved with compassion, he dismounted, gave a cup of water to the suffering man, and the cup glowed with fire as if it were alive with the joys of the new Covenant of Love. The Knight found the Holy Grail, not in deeds of prowess, but in hospitality to the needy.

Wells are made sweeter for the drawing. Those from which no one draws water for beast and fellow human being become polluted. Riches too become more peaceful when used as fuel for charity. The poor cannot reward us for hospitality; therefore God will have to do so. It was these He asked us to invite to our dinners, and it is interesting to note that He always called them, not meals but "banquets."

HAPPINESS

13. Joy and Sadness

The wise man said: "Cast sadness far from thee, because it has killed many, and is good for nothing." There is hardly anything as apt to bring our hearts to a state of irksome disgust as sadness. Those who have made a psychological study of sadness tell us that one of its principal effects is to disturb our judgments, making us take a darker view of life than the facts justify. Thus, sadness leads to pessimism and the reverse effect is also true — all pessimists are necessarily sad: disaster, for them, is just around the corner. A second effect of sadness is to make us rude to others and severe towards them, suspicious and ready to put the worst interpretation on the actions of everyone around us.

There are different ways of trying to overcome the sense of sadness. Some people take recourse to alcohol to make them forget. Others fling themselves into carnal pleasures hoping that the intensity of a momentary thrill will compensate them for a want of a goal and a purpose in life. But all sad people are alike in this: at some time they say — perhaps scarcely conscious that they are saying it — "I do not love myself." This is not an "inferiority complex." It is rather the higher part of the self looking down on the lower part and reprimanding it for its pitiable condition. Animals cannot reflect on themselves as human beings do; hence they cannot feel the same kind of disgust.

There is a remedy for sadness — the one suggested by the Scriptures. To some minds it may seem farfetched, when it says: "If you are suffering, pray!" (Jm 5:13). Actually, these words touch on a profound psychological truth, for they imply that we must be reconciled to ourselves in order to be happy. So long as we are merely the battleground of a war between the lower self and the higher self within us, there can be no relaxation and no joy. But to resolve the conflict, to bring the battle to an end, we must see ourselves as we really are. It does no good to blame the golf club if our game is at fault, or the pitcher because we spill the milk, the fault must be seen as our own in little mishaps of this kind, and for our states of mind as well. The discovery that we are to blame for being the way we are is greater than the discovery made by any explorer — such a discovery of our own fault is impossible unless there be a higher standard outside ourselves, from whose love we know that we have fallen.

When our own responsibility for our sadness has once been faced, prayer next leads us on to hope, because it shows us the real basis for our discontent: the knowledge that we could be quite different from the way we are. As one writer put it: "I was told that I was the offspring of a father and a mother.

I had thought that I was more." And one is more. The Savior said that each one of us is of more worth than the whole visible universe (cf. Mt 10:31 and Lk 12:6)!

We begin to act differently when we recognize the immensity of our possibilities. Our whole life changes then, like that of a farmer when he discovers oil on what he had previously believed to be just a poor farm. Prayer overcomes sadness by putting us in relation with the Eternal, and then the change occurs. Before, we had thought ourselves unloved by anyone; now, we know that we are loved by God.

Unless we put God between ourselves and our previous life, we cannot hope to make real spiritual progress. But God does not give Himself to us until we have begun to feel our own nothingness. By assenting to the poverty of our personality we open the floodgates of Divine riches. It has been said that no one is a hero to his valet. It would be truer to say that no one is a hero to himself. Plutarch may tell us that Cato was a great human being; but to Cato, Cato was weak.

It is one thing to discover one's nothingness, and to rest there — that is sadness. It is quite another thing to discover that one is nothing, and from there to make use of the Divine Energies — that is joy. Mediocrity is a sin against ourselves, a kind of sacrilege. The *ennui* some hearts feel is nothing but the instinctive reaction of their great and undeveloped possibilities in the face of the triviality and mediocrity of their lives. All around us, birds are flying, musical in song, eager to enter into our souls. But until we are reconciled with the goal of life, they have to be content to perch on the top of our roof for a moment, and then fly away.

To pass from sadness to joy requires a birth, a moment of travail and labor, for no one ever mounts to a higher level of life without death to the lower. Before such an ascent, conscience, for a moment, has a hard, stern work to do. Pearls come from the bottom of the water, gold from the depths of the earth, and the great joys of life are to be found in the recesses of a contrite, broken heart.

Joy is the happiness of love — love aware of its own inner happiness. Pleasure comes from without, but joy comes from within, and it is, therefore, within the reach of everyone in the world. For if there is sadness in our hearts it is because there is not enough love. But to be loved, we must be lovable; to be lovable, we must he good, to be good, we must know Goodness, and to know Goodness is to love God, and neighbor, and everybody in the world.

14. Mystery of Suffering

God breathes on us in our joys; He whispers in our conscience; He speaks in our troubles; and He shouts in our pains. Suffering is too great a mystery for reason to fully comprehend its meaning; its understanding demands a loftiness of soul and surrender of spirit which few are prepared to make.

Pain and suffering seem to be closely linked up with the cosmos itself, as if by some great free decision on our part the peace and concord of life were disturbed. Our solar system itself began with some great travail and labor of a major disturbance; our own planet had its ice age, with great waters vomiting themselves through hills and mountains, and our earth has its tumultuous change of seasons.

When we consider the human condition, we find that there are two kinds of sufferings: the pure and the impure. The impure pains are those which come from without through no fault of our own, such as plagues, disease, accidents, etc. Pure pain is that which comes from ourselves, such as physical pains resulting from an abuse of the laws of health: excesses in drinking, or worries, anxious fears caused by violations of the moral law.

It must never be thought that, because one suffers, therefore one is guilty or is being punished. In a general way, the disorders and evils of the world do follow from man planting a rebel's flag against the Creator; but it can never be said in any individual case the suffering was due to personal guilt. The Christ Who died on the Cross did nothing wrong. The innocent can suffer as well as the guilty.

More important is the question: what can one do in the face of pain and suffering? Various solutions have been offered. One is Stoicism, which is to grit one's teeth and bear it, in order to prove apathy and indifference to the ills of the world; another way is that of Buddhism, which is to see all suffering as the result of desire. As one crushes desire and strives for union with the great Nirvana of unconsciousness, one diminishes and finally conquers suffering. The Old Testament, as revealed in the Book of Job, is to acknowledge that we are face to face with a mystery which is incapable of solution by reason. When Job asks God questions, God appears and begins asking Job questions, such as, "Where were you when I laid the foundations of the earth?" When God finished asking Job questions, Job realized that the questions of God made more sense than the answers of men. Job's final philosophy was summed up in his words: "Slay me though he might, I will trust in him" (Job 13:15).

The Christian answer is that evil is due basically to sin. Hence the way to conquer suffering is to conquer sin. To do so, the Son of God took on Himself a human nature. Identifying Himself with us, He took on also our guilt as a father takes on the debts of a wayward son. Being human, He could suffer as one of us, and in our name; being God, His sufferings would have infinite value, and blot out all the debts we owed. The Resurrection was the final manifestation that the love of God is stronger than the power of sin. If pain and suffering were insoluble, the Heavenly Father would never have fitted it into the pattern of His Divine Son.

The lesson is that perfection is attained through work, sacrifice, and self-denial. Sometimes it is self-imposed, and at other times imposed by others; then it becomes necessary to patiently bear the Cross in love of Him Who died for us. A mother gives a child bitter medicine; though the child protests, he knows it comes from a loving hand and for his own good. Love cannot extinguish suffering, but it can diminish it, as love makes an all night vigil by her sick child seem less hard. Where there is this assurance that love suffered for us to atone for our sins, we can find peace in resigning ourselves to the Divine Will. As Dante said: "In His will is our peace" (*Divine Comedy*, "Paradiso," canto III, Line 85). Franz Werfel, continuing that idea, gave this motto to peacemakers: "Not revenge, but expiation; not punishment, but penance."

15. Our Moods

Our Blessed Lord advised us: "When you fast, do not be sad or wear a long face as the hypocrites do" (Mt 6:16). Then He cautioned His hearers to so dress themselves that no one would know they were fasting. Sadness is atheistic; it is not Christian. It is atheistic not only because it shows a lack of faith, leaving one with no invisible means of support, but also because it robs one of hope as day adds to day and the lease on life runs out. Many who have an empty stomach or a trial on the inside, placard it on their faces, register it in their voices and show it in their actions. Their disposition is either morose, taciturn, moody, grouchy, bitter or sharp. In a word, they are sad.

All has not gone well at the office, or in the factory. The husband returns and answers his wife in monosyllables, if he answers her at all. The phone rings and a customer is at the other end, all is sweetness and light. This disproves those who say that bad humor is really not our fault at all, it is due to getting up on the wrong side of he bed, or "my rheumatism is bothering me today," or "my corn hurts and I know it is going to rain." These excuses are the same as those given in universities for sins, such as blaming it on our genes, or on society, or on the stars. The truth of the matter is, as Shakespeare says,

"The fault... is not in our stars, but in ourselves" (*Julius Caesar*, Act I, Scene ii, Line 134). External circumstances may condition our mental outlook and our dispositions, but they do not cause them.

Just as there is a right and wrong theory about the sun and the earth, so there is a right and wrong theory about external circumstances. If we revolve about what happens on the outside, then the latter determines our moods and attitudes. But if we make what is external revolve around us, we can determine the amount of their influence. Either what is outside makes our moods, or our moods determine our outlook on what is outside us. The pot that over-boils can boil over the temper, or the temper can see the pot over-boil and not get mad. Continuing that figure, it may be said that there are some people who in a quarrel love to keep the "pot boiling."

Rainy days do make some people sad, but the author remembers saying once to a resident of Killarney: "Too bad it's raining." He answered: "But it's a good day to save your soul." Come to think about it, it may be easier to do that on rainy days than on sunny days. Our humor and disposition are not so much the reflection of the weather or the wrong side of the bed, as they are the reflections of the state of our soul. What is outside of us is beyond our control; but what is within us can be mastered and woven to any desired pattern. As Pascal once said: "Time and my moods have little relationship; I have my fogs and my bad weather within me." Our personal dispositions are as window panes through which we see the world either as rosy or dull. The way we color the glasses we wear is the way the world seems to us. To a great extent what we see is colored from the inside, rather than from the outside.

Two considerations are helpful in developing a good disposition. The first is to be mindful that a happy conscience makes a happy outlook on life, and an unhappy conscience makes us miserable on the inside and everyone else miserable on the outside. When our conscience bothers us, whether we admit it or not, we often try to justify it by correcting others, or by finding fault with them. The readiness to believe evil about others is in a large part ammunition for a thousand scandals in our own hearts. But by finding black spots in others, they believe they distract attention from their own miserable state. The good conscience, on the contrary, finds good in others even when there is some discontent with self.

The second aid to good humor is the spirit of joy. Joy is rejoicing in another's progress. This is one of the rarest virtues and the last to be won. Too often the progress of others is regarded as stolen from self. A man loses his good humor when he calls his wife "dear" when they are out and an "ox" when at home. The wife loses her joy when she would rather spend her time mending his ways than mending his socks. All have joy when they thank God that their friends have done good work, that they are loved by others, and that their virtues proclaim the joy of a good conscience.

16. Mental Cases Are Increasing

Human beings have always taken for granted that there would be in their midst a few unfortunate individuals whose mental outlook would be warped and unpredictable. But what is disturbing today is the number of otherwise normal people who, in popular language, are "cracking up." Some are young, otherwise happily married; others are in middle life, with apparent security; but, regardless of the age group, as a good American psychiatrist wrote, "Mental cases are the stepchild of modern civilization."

Leaving to the medical profession those who are suffering from functional and organic disturbances which affect the mind, our problem is to inquire into the reason for the many marginal or fringe cases of mental instability. Coming quickly to the point, it appears to be this: Our generation has been raised on the idea of "self-expression," which, being translated negatively, means there should never be any self-restraint. Every desire and impulse which satisfies the ego is considered good; any form of self-denial, or repression of biological urges, is considered as harmful to the personality. The ego is flattered and pampered, even to a point where children are raised on the theory that they should never be disciplined, much less punished or reprimanded for their selfishness.

When a person builds his philosophy of life on the principle of self-will, he is in for a tremendous shock. It happens that most other people he meets in the world have exactly the same principle. The result is that one individual has his self-will contradicted by another; the ego is negated by another ego; wishes are not fulfilled; whims are negated, crossed and rejected by other egos equally bent on self assertion.

This constant battering and challenge from other wills makes the mind confused, fills it with the sense of being persecuted, creates unhappiness, revenge and spitefulness.

Some seek professional advice regarding their confused mental state, and are told that they are suffering from an "inferiority complex." The truth of the matter is, nobody who is self-willed has an inferiority complex; he has a superiority complex. He is so full of conceit, pride and aggressive assertiveness that his hurt feelings may for the moment appear as inferiority. But he would not feel hurt if he did not have a diabolic pride, or superiority which would treat anyone who does not flatter him as Pontius Pilate treated Christ. Pilate washed his hands of Christ and had Him executed.

The hour has come for educators, sociologists and citizens to reverse their steps, to see that if the self is to be really happy, it must be disciplined, pruned, denied and negated by itself. No better law for inner peace has ever been given than that of the Divine Savior: "*If any one will come after Me, let him take up his cross daily and follow Me*" (Lk 9:23). In other words, crosses and contradictions are a part of life. We are to expect them from others simply because they are often as unregenerate as ourselves. Contradictions from others will hurt us less when we have first contradicted ourselves. The hand that is calloused will not pain as much as a soft hand, on catching a hard ball. Contradictions can even be assimilated and used for further taming our own errant impulses.

But the will that always insists on having its own way, begins to hate its own way. Those who live only for self begin to hate self. Self is too narrow, confining and dark a sanctuary for happy adoration.

Crosses are inescapable. Those who start with self-love have already created for themselves the possibility of millions of other crosses from those who live by the same pride. But those who discipline themselves and tame the ego by little acts of self-denial have already prepared themselves to meet crosses from the outside; they have familiarized themselves with them, and the shock is less when they are thrust on their shoulders.

There are only two things we can do with crosses — carry them or kick against them. We can merge them in God's plan for life and thus make them serve our inner peace and happiness, or we can stumble over them to the glen of weeping. Selfishness is the cause of much mental sickness; otherness, sympathy, forgiveness and self-discipline are the cure.

17. Melancholy

Melancholy is a strictly modern phenomenon, made by the wings of the soul beating against the bars of the cage of time. The greatest analyst on this subject, Sören Kierkegaard, once expressed his own personal melancholy as follows: "I have just returned from a party of which I was the life and soul. Wit poured from my lips, everyone laughed and admired me — but I left — and the dash should be as long as the earth's orbit — and wanted to shoot myself."

This type of melancholy is not so much due to the burdens of life as it is to a reaction from its pleasures. Nero, one of the greatest of all sensualists, was notoriously melancholic. In more religious days of the past the pleasure addict had remorse, which implied conscience. But melancholy, unlike remorse, is devoid of conscious ethical consideration; it is an emptiness that comes from having spent too riotously the honeyed pleasures of the body; it is a horrifying sense of barren activity, romantic nothingness, and the futility of life itself. Those who are unhappy try to escape by losing themselves in excitements, stimulants and erotic experiences. But instead of any of these being a bed where they may feather their nest in repose, each turns out to be a rubber wall which makes them rebound upon themselves. The very self from which they sought release is now the very self which tortures them. The more they try to lose themselves, the more they find themselves. They breathe in the same air they breathed out, and each time it becomes more polluted and less bearable.

Melancholy thus produces what might be called "re-duplication." The self is confronted with self. A prisoner escaped one night from a prison, walked all night, swam a river twice, and at sunup found himself back at the very prison from which he escaped. The melancholic is like this: he is always trying to "get away from himself," but all the roads he takes are circular and he meets himself coming back. It is not a pleasing sensation, any more than the first glance in the mirror on awakening. There is the inescapable "thou" and the "I," and there hardly seems to be room for both in the apartment of the soul. Those without a goal in life go fishing for pleasure and on the hook they catch themselves not in enjoyment but in disillusionment and suffering.

At this point, one of two things may happen. First, a person may become *defiant* about his despair and, if he is an author, may write a drama or a novel proving that melancholy is the lot of humanity. Having burned his hand on the fires of egotism, he may seek relief by describing burns as normal and conflagrations as hearths where hearts may warm themselves. Evil is always easier to write about than goodness, because all people have some experience of evil, but not all have a major experience in virtue. The nightmares of despair and melancholy that provide themes for the stage and movies bear witness to the frustration in many modern souls and to their ineffectual attempts at purgation by spreading the epidemic.

But there is another possible reaction to melancholy than defiance, and that is realizing that one is locked in a combat with self. As soon as one sees that his mind is a battlefield in which the personality which is split is waging a war, one begins to look for a peacemaker. The "two have to get together," used so often in speaking of social and international disputes, is now applied to self. Obviously, peace cannot come from within, for that is the source of all the trouble. The mind is like a willow tree whose branches are already wet with tears. As the sun alone can dry the dampness of the tree, so now the melancholic mind looks *outside* self for help and deliverance.

And this is the way many a modern mind is finding God, through the emptiness of self and the despair within. It has always been known that a person could come to God through a series of disgusts, but it remained for our day to form it into a pattern. The contradiction within, which drives the defiant melancholic individual to suicide, is the same force which drives the self-acknowledged melancholic to God. Sartre is the world's spokesman for the despair that prefaces hell, and Kierkegaard the spokesman for those who in the darkness of their self-sealed tombs cry for light. The modern mind has been closed to God for a long time, but it seems now that God is finding His way back as He did at the beginning of Christian history — coming once more through closed doors!

18. The Fault Is In Ourselves

Politics is what might be called "deferred repentance" — the keeping clean of the outside of the cup in order to escape the necessity of cleaning the inside. The great appeal of so many modern political philosophies is that they make all the evils of the world economic, and thus dispense its victims from the need of moral betterment. There is more fun in pointing out the splinter in another's eye than in picking the girder out of one's own. Those ages which have an inordinate interest in the reformation of society are often those who are most heedless of the reformation of the individual. That group of educators who say that evil is nonexistent and that there are only complexes are like those who say that there are no diseases in the body, but only imaginations.

The fact is that every person can be egotistic and selfish, and in such a case there is no one except himself to blame. It is not just the desire for economic well-being or for security that makes a person anti-social, it is most often his desire to have his own way — come what may. Hilaire Belloc told the story of a man trundling a large vat of wine on a cart, and as he passed through one village after another, he haggled with prospective purchasers about the price. In the end he hands out the drink to everyone for nothing. It was not so much gain he wanted; it was his own way.

In the parable of the prodigal son, the son broke first with his father in his heart, and then wanted the division of goods. The economic division was merely a consequence of the alienation of his heart from his father. The full economic life is no barrier to a break with the tradition of home, country and religion. Sometimes the abundance of the material leads men to believe that happiness is to be found without, rather than within.

The prodigal son, after suffering from a famine in a foreign country, was restored to a sense of values when "he came to himself." That reality broke in upon him; he saw that nothing outside, but something inside himself was the root of all his troubles. But here is an absorbing psychological fact. When an egotist begins to see that he is to blame for his condition, there is apt to be a moment which exasperates him into open rebellion; at this stage, the egotist is not immoral in action; he is anti-moral and anti-religious in his attitudes, words and thoughts. Shame and a false remorse have madded him to a moral Laocoon stung into a living martyrdom by the serpents in his bosom. Much of the bigotry and the attacks hurled against decency by exhausted libertines spring from the soul's first passionate recoil against detected criminality, discovered viciousness, or stained honor. The intolerable anguish of a wounded egotist, in which he is whipped not by whips but by scorpions, prompts him to attacks on morality, from which before conscience began whipping him, he would have shrunk with horror. Perhaps if we understood human nature better, we would see that those who hate goodness and decency violently are also those who hate themselves more; they relieve for a time the pressure for interior reformation and compensate for it by outrages against that which they know to be true, but refuse to embrace. For the same reason, those who are filled with hate and are anti-God may be closer to genuine piety than those of our modern Western world who are neither hot nor cold and, therefore, will be vomited from the mouth of God. Few hells are deeper than when a disillusioned egotist and an evil conscience boil together in the same cauldron.

One of the classic stories of antiquity is Circe, who transformed human beings into swine, or lowered humanity into the state of brute beasts. Circe today parades under the name of a psychology which reduces the human being to an animal. But there was also an Ulysses who compelled the enchantress to restore his companions into that former shape. Our world of education and psychology needs someone to do that, to make us conscious of our true identity, to restore the egotist to sanity. This is the grace of Christ which brings prodigals from the pigsty back to the Father's house.

EXTERNAL INFLUENCES

19. Influence

With some measure of pessimism, Shakespeare makes one of his characters say: "The evil that men do lives after them, the good is oft interred with their bones" (*Julius Caesar*, Act III, Scene ii, Line 79). More hopeful was the poet who wrote: "Full lasting is the song, though he the singer, passes" (George Meredith, *The Thrush in February*, st. 17). Both, however, are in agreement on the importance of influence, either for evil or for good. Some can look back and fix the day when a good influence began and say with Dante: "In that part of the book of my memory, before which is little that can be read, there is a rubric, saying, 'The new life begins'" (*La Vita Nuova*, tr. by Dante Gabriel Rossetti). In the gallery of memory, some portrait is hanging to which one can acknowledge a debt of formation, or a fresh vision of life.

Influences are of two kinds: conscious and unconscious. Conscious influence is one in which we deliberately seek to mould the character or the mentality of another. This kind of influence is not always sound, it is too closely related to advertising. Almost all the great impacts on the characters of others have been made indirectly, not directly. He who starts out to "edify" others almost always makes a fool of himself. That is why poses of piety, going out of one's way to appear religious, or the citation of texts of Scripture to impress have a ring of insincerity about them. Our Divine Lord condemned those who went about saying, "Lord, Lord" (Mt 7:21), because such lip worship did not mean a person was thereby a member of the Kingdom of God.

Whenever we set out to give "good example," we generally do not give it. The best example is given when we are off duty and are not acting "professionally," such as the minister or rabbi or priest when he comes down from his pulpit, the womanizer after he has finished his discourse on the "necessity of recognizing the rights of women," the politician when he has finished his television oration on "my profound interest in social justice and my love of the common good." When Peter told Our Lord that though others failed Him, he would never fail, the Savior retorted that within twenty-four hours Peter would deny that he even knew Him. What we say is less important in the way of influence than what we do.

The best influences in life are undeliberate, unconscious; when no one is watching, or when reaction to the good deed was never sought. Such is the long-range influence of a mother in a home; fulfilling of daily duties with love and a spirit of self-sacrifice leaves an imprint on the children that deepens with the years. St. Francis has done much to influence painting, though he was not an artist.

Great artists have influenced millions to love beauty, though their intention was never to be so remembered. Unconscious influence is never superior. As Our Divine Lord said: "I am among you as One Who serves" (Lk 22:27). From that basic humility came the advice to His disciples, that one who would be the greatest among them should be the least of all (Mt 23:11). At the same time, He was never so royal as when He committed Himself to death in order to save others.

The unfortunate characteristic of our day is that propaganda has taken the place of personal influence. Politics has become so primary in modern life, that the masses are more moved by promises than by fulfillments. Communism swept one-third of the world into the grasp of the Iron Bear simply because it promised pie in the sky after hatred had overthrown the existing order. The great fallacy of all revolutionary movements is that the value of great lives is nullified, either through persecution or character assassination, in the interests of fallacious promises and illusory hopes. Our world is slow to learn that those who turn out the lights of heaven, by that very act turn out the lights of earth. *Influences* are born of moral stamina but promises, like spider webs, are woven from the bellies of materialism.

Some day a politician will arise who will be so devoted to truth that he will follow it, knowing that by doing so he will go down to defeat. That day will be the restoration of politics as principles; it will also be the rebirth of a nation.

20. Bread and Kings

People talk most about their health when they are sick, and most about liberty when they are in danger of losing it. Despite all the pleas for liberty, it must be remembered that every flight from responsibility is a flight from liberty and every denial of personal guilt is also a denial of freedom. Cabbages cannot do wrong, though they have heads; calculators cannot commit sin, though they can do many things which seem to emulate human thought. Perhaps it is the very burden of responsibility which flows from free choice that makes so many human beings ready to surrender their great gift of freedom. This also explains the search for someone to whom they can commit their choice, who will do their thinking for them and relieve them of the awful burden of the consequences of their free decisions. This search for someone to whom neurotic minds can commit themselves explains the comparatively facile surrender of so many to totalitarianism in our day and age.

Two Russian writers of the nineteenth century foretold that this state of affairs would come to pass in the twentieth century; one of them predicted that the leaders to whom free minds would surrender themselves would come from Russia. Soloviev said that the leader who would captivate souls in our generation would be the author of a book on "Peace and Security for the World." Millions would submit to him as the supreme authority in the political and economic sphere for no other reason than because he promised bread. Dostoievski also foretold that Russia and the world would fall to the "temptation of bread and power."

One cannot help but contrast this search for a dictator or an economic king with Our Blessed Lord when He fed the bread to the multitudes in the desert. Having fed the hungry masses, they "sought to make Him king" (Jn 6:15). It is ever in the human heart, when it loses its love of the spiritual, to worship those who promise full stomachs or economic power. They wished to make Jesus king in opposition to all the kings of the earth; instead of surrendering themselves to Him and His sublime doctrine about sin and redemption, they willed to have Him submit to them. They did not want to be drawn up to Him, but to draw Him down to them. However sincere and enthusiastic they were, they were, nevertheless, bent on pulling Divinity down to the level of the human.

Though He Who was rich became poor for our sake, yet He would not be an earthly king by force. A poor blind man could stop Him on the roadway to be cured of his blindness, but not all the masses with their universal acclaim and suffrage could make Him king. Then He laid His finger on their error: "You seek Me not because you saw signs, but because you ate of the loaves and were satisfied" (Jn 6:26). They sought Him not for the higher part of their being, but for their stomachs; not for His morality, but for their economics; not for His saving grace, but because of the dormancy of the spiritual in their souls.

When loaves are more valued than the Divine Power which multiplied them; when streams are more admired than the fountains that produced them, the world will accept any kind of a king who promises bread and plenty. Nor let it be forgotten that He Who promised the spiritual did not deny bread to the poor. Our hopes and our liberties are sold too cheap when they are bartered away to him who feeds the body and leaves the soul unsatisfied. This is the problem: The whole world is dying of hunger — the Eastern world is dying of hunger of body; the Western world is dying of hunger of soul. The first will be fed, but not by those who hate liberty when they give them flour; the Western world will be saved by feeding the East while recognizing their own hunger of the Spirit and by seeking again

the true King of Hearts Who alone gives "The Bread
of Life."

21. Passion

Listening to a political figure give a television report
to the nation on a world crisis with somewhat the
same passion that he would read off the price of
cheese in Switzerland and Burma makes one wonder if there is any fire or enthusiasm left for great
causes. Obviously, enthusiasm has something to do
with passion. But that word generally evokes two
kinds of extreme and wrong reactions: one view is
that passion is something we ought to be ashamed
of; the other is that passion is always right, and that
if we do not give way to its demands, we hurt our
personality.

To revive passion in hearts, one must first
understand it. Passion signifies receiving or suffering something or submitting to something. From
this, follow two indispensable conditions for passion: knowledge, and some organic or physical
change in our sensible nature.

First, knowledge. Passion cannot operate unless we have an idea about something. A woman will
not "get mad" at a bargain counter, unless she knows

that someone is getting the better selection. We speak of people becoming "enthused" about some idea — and an idea is knowledge. No one undergoes the passion of sadness without first having a knowledge of a loss or a disaster.

Second, passion has its seat in the body or the animal nature of man. It is the echo of the knowledge in our physical structure but it is not knowledge. Passion implies sensible changes, such as the flushing of the cheeks, the dilating of the pupils and the tensing of many of the muscles.

Passion is not a reflex like the watering of a dog's mouth in the presence of food. It is true that there are many similarities between passion in animals and passion in man, but it must never be forgotten that in man, passion cannot operate unless something is known. The eye has a reflex action when someone is about to thrust his finger into it, but passion is a conscious affair; it is something that happens to a creature endowed with reason and free will.

The next point to remember is that at the root of all passions are love and its opposite, hate. Hence our passions are either for the pursuit of what we love, or escape from what we hate. Because we love sleep, we can immediately think of certain passions that would be aroused because we were denied it, e.g., anger, at the porter on the train who called us two hours too early; despair, when we cannot get to sleep at night; hope, that the visitors who dropped in "for a few minutes" will not stay "for a few hours." I know of someone who at ten o'clock puts on a night cap, walks through the living room and facetiously bids every one good night. Because we hate certain things, other passions which are related to struggle with difficulties also arise; for example, fear that we may not have enough security for old age, flight from a mad dog, etc.

Coming back to want of fire and enthusiasm in our politicians, the reason is rather obvious. They have no great central overwhelming cause to which they are dedicated with the full fervor of their being, and they have no great shock at evil or wrong. Nothing has so much killed enthusiasm as the pragmatic notion that there is nothing that is absolutely true, right, and good for which one ought to consecrate his life; and there is nothing so evil that one ought to die rather than surrender to it. Indifference kills passions; while skepticism deadens them. Democracy does not mean that because both sides ought to be heard, therefore there is no right side. There are two sides to fly paper. There are passions where there are ideas that lead to action. Democracy today finds it hard to make up its mind on what is right. Communism, on the contrary, made up its mind on what was wrong. All its passions were devoted to evil. Evil today is starting the fires that are burning down the world. Leadership in democracies today cannot be expected to come out of the ashes of spineless indifference. When more get mad, not because they lose money, but because right is ignored and wrong enthroned, then the fires will come back to democracy. And these fires will burn like beacons summoning men to a finer and better world.

22. Five Fish for the Devil's Hooks

As one makes a study of those who have been caught on the hooks of the Devil's fishing line, or who hide behind their freedoms in order to destroy the very source of that freedom, and who are thus particularly gullible for the Devil's bait can be reduced to five classes.

1. *Haters.* Bigots use their heads, though wrongly; haters use their spleens, though overmuch. Hate may come from being ridiculed, for having lost a job, or for being unsuccessful. In order to exonerate themselves, they fasten the blame on others, and develop an unholy hate against a class, a race, a government, a party, a business organization, a group or a Church. But, since their individual hate has such impotence, they search about for some conspiracy that will socialize their resentment. Find-

ing a group which collectivizes and intensifies their hatred, they swallow the hook, not so much because of what they admire in the group, but because of what they hate outside the group which socializes their hatred.

2. *Socializers*. Not everyone in our modern world develops social interests because he loves his neighbor in God. There are some who enter social work in order to escape the incessant accusing repartee of their consciences. Failing in individual justice, they compensate for it by espousing social justice; they escape the need of personal reformation by going hog wild about social reformation; they meddle with everyone else's morals, in order to be too busy to correct their own. If their behavior were better, they would be truly religious people and do much good for society. They look for a cause which will leave them alone with their individual vices. They swallow the Devil's line also because its anti-religious character satisfies their desire to expunge from the world all ideas of morality and virtue, the infractions against which have made them so uneasy in the dark.

3. *Bored Intelligentsia*. Their education should have given them a goal or a purpose of life. Having failed to do so, their knowledge is nothing but a crazy quilt of unrelated facts and undigested bits of information. The want of unity both in their moral life and their knowledge makes them desirous of

unity, but not a unity from *within* which demands moral stamina, but a unity from *without*. Certain sects provide that for them. They no longer have to think; the sect does the thinking for them. They now have a mission, a sense of belonging to a totality, and one in which they are no longer bored by their freedom, having surrendered it to the collective ant hill of the sect.

Intelligentsia do not become members of a sect for an intellectual reason. That is why when discussing the sect with them, they never seem to understand it. Instead of a "reason" for becoming a member, they have only an "intention," namely the desire to escape boredom. Their motives are alien to the rational.

4. *Neurotics*. Every neurotic is anti-social. Normal persons are linked to society; the abnormal, uprooted through their delusions, are daily confronted with the absurd. They are "naturals" for any anti-social movement opposed to culture, morality and peace. In fact the more absurd a system is, the more it appeals to them. The connection between the neurotic anti-social traits of a person and the neurotic anti-social wars and revolutions which we see around us in the world today is extremely close. As flies go to honey, so neurotics gravitate to anti-social behavior. They are easy targets for the Devil's bait.

5. *Satellites*. These are just plain dupes or

"dopes." They may not be obedient in *action*, but they are obedient in *thought*. They see only what they want to see; they love the limelight which certain causes give them, but are incapable of analyzing an historical situation. They are professional signers; they will put their name to anything that identifies liberty with license. The Devil uses them because they are naive and credulous. They belong to every "politically correct" organization, but like the false fronts waiters wear, they are nothing but stuffed shirts — with a tail which the Devil twists to his own good pleasure.

VIRTUE

23. Selflessness

We all pass through three stages: youth, middle age, and maturity. Each has its corresponding passion, which would destroy or impair personality by making it a slave to something low or base. The passion of youth is sex; the passion of middle age is power or ambition; the passion of the mature is avarice. These passions are not base in themselves — no passion ever is. They become base only when consented to against right reason and the Law of God.

Those who consent to the deordinations of the flesh in youth often sublimate into the ambitious in the forties, and to avaricious in the sixties. The object of their passion has changed, but they have not. In one instance, the object is the body in the other the ego or the proud mind, and in the last instance, things (wealth) outside both body and mind. The first excess of the flesh is generally recognized as wrong, but modern civilization does not regard pride or avarice as "dirty" sins, though they can be just as disastrous as lust.

Of the three, lust, egotism, and greed, the first is the easiest for the spirit to master, because its excesses create its own emptiness. Sated flesh-love can create a desire for spirit-love. But egotism and greed are very difficult to cure, because they are *inflationary* sins. Excesses of flesh deflate, but pride and wealth swell the ego to a point where we can come to believe we are truly great, either because we think we are, or because we judge ourselves by what we *have*, rather than by what we *are*.

Since egotism, pride and selfishness are so dominant in middle age, it is important to concentrate on their judgment. One day when the Apostles were quarreling among themselves as to who was the greatest among them, Our Lord placed a child in the midst of them, as an example that the littlest is the greatest (cf. Mk 9:35). Later, He followed this act with the words: "Let the greatest among you be like the youngest, and the ruler like one who serves" (Lk 22:26).

By the Divine standard, true greatness is indicated neither by the possession of great abilities nor the buzz of popular applause. Any talent a person has, such as a talent for singing, speaking, or writing, is a gift of God. He has done nothing more to merit it than a child with a beautiful face. "If then, you have received it, why do you boast as if it were yours alone?" (1 Cor 4:7). The richer the gifts, the greater the responsibilities on the day of Judgment.

When Our Divine Lord said that the great must be as the least, He made the measure of greatness usefulness and service to one's neighbor in His Name. Service of others is necessary because it involves the constant repression of those egotistic tendencies in us which exalt us at the expense of others. Aristotle said that the two most degrading tendencies in a human being were towards bad temper and ill-regulated desire. Either one or the other is present in every egotist. He either gets mad at others because they do not praise him or do his will, or he seeks his own pleasure at the expense and shame of others.

Service corrects both of these evil tendencies. It removes ill-temper by making the person do good to others out of obedience to God's Will. A man in love with a woman conceals his ill-temper to win her love. A soul in love with God kills his ill-temper to be worthy of the love of God. Service also corrects ill-regulated desires by constantly putting the needs of the neighbor before the wishes of the ego. They are selfless because absorbed in other selves; happy because they have no needs except to bestow on their fellow men the overflowing goodness of their hearts. And such selfless souls are always the most popular in offices, schools, clubs, factories and playgrounds.

What a lesson nature teaches about selflessness! Clouds, playing like lambs in the pastures of the sky, never keep their treasures of moisture to themselves, but pour them out in the beautiful benediction of rain to a thirsty earth. No drop of water leads a selfish life. There is no breeze without its mission. Human lives were not sent into this world as ornaments. God has prettier things for that purpose. As the bird that sings for others gladdens its own heart with song, as the rivers flee the decay of stagnant self-content to service the mighty ocean, as the sun burns itself out to light a world, so does everything — man included — become good by doing good to others.

But if we are to do good to others, they must be loved for God's sake. No moral profit comes from doing good to another because "she can get it for us wholesale" or from giving gifts to others because of the pleasure they give us. There is not even great merit in doing good to those who love us. "If you love those who love you, what reward is there in that? Do not sinners do the same?" (Lk 6:32). The greatest spiritual profit comes from loving those who hate us, and from giving gifts and dinners to those who cannot give anything in return, for then recompense will be made in the Kingdom of Heaven (cf. Lk 14:12-14).

The inertia of selfish idleness and of greed will best be overcome on our knees, praying for the entrance of the Spirit of Love. The mill-wheel stops when the rushing waters are stilled; the moving train stops when the hot embers cool; and charity vanishes as the love of God declines. If people only knew how happy they would make themselves if they really helped their neighbor for the love of God, we would soon become a nation with songs in our hearts, as well as on our lips.

24. Insincerity

It is quite generally taken for granted that the way to be popular is to say things you do not mean, or to draw a veil between your mind and your lips, or divorce thoughts from actions. Their lips then carry honeyed speech; their hands carry stilettos; the speech is for other ears; the stilettos are for others' backs. Psychologically, those who manifestly are shams are generally known through three techniques: first they shake hands with you up to the elbow, and they thrust their face against your nose with a smile which seems to say, "See how nice I am," or they shout out their greeting in tones calculated to make volume substitute for honesty.

Children do not have this duplicity because they are natural and it is acquired. If their mother tells them to tell a stranger at the door that she is not at home, they will invariably say, "My mother told me to tell you that she is not at home." I know of a mother who, after an introduction to several ladies who had dropped in for tea, asked her child, "Now which one did I say was my best friend?" The child in the presence of all answered, "The one with the big teeth." It takes some falling away from the childlike simplicity that purchases heaven, before one develops the film of dishonesty.

There are moments when it is very difficult to

express one's views, for example, when a husband is asked how he likes his wife's new hat, or how he likes her new Italian haircut — which to him resembles unstrung spaghetti. Women, when faced with something they do not like, generally go into ecstasies of praise in order to cover up their real mind. Men generally descend to monosyllables or a long grunt. When a man gets mad at his wife at cards he generally calls her "dear" but with such a coolness as to make her think she is a "Frigidear." Tact, in such difficult moments, does not mean lying, nor smoothness at the expense of truth, but it does mean circumspection. Some women, on being asked how they like another woman's dress, will generally say that it is "lovely," but the tone of the voice betrays the suspicion that it is not.

The opposite form of insincerity is flattery. As we have said before, there are two kinds of flattery: blarney and baloney. Blarney is the varnished truth; baloney is the unvarnished lie. Blarney is flattery laid on so thin, you like it; baloney is flattery laid on so thick, you hate it. As Shakespeare said, "that was laid on with a trowel" (*As You Like It*, Act I, Scene ii, Line 113). The amount of flattery one spreads on another depends either on how much one wishes to exalt his own ego, or on how much one wishes to deceive the ego of the hearer. Rare are those who use such restraint in flattery in order to delude others into asking them to "say that again."

Because it is perhaps all too true of those in high places, the following doggerel is laughingly told:

To the Bishop as he mounted
for the first time to his throne
bent the princely Consecrator
with his confidential tone:
Two things only in this office
merit certainty, forsooth:
Nevermore to pay for dinner.
Nevermore to hear the truth.

Insincerity of a minor degree is that in which we constantly promise something that we never expect to fulfill. The "Yes Man" is Exhibit A of that group, who is always afraid to assert his own mind and who identifies agreement with agreeableness. Another form is the invitation to dinner, "Come up and have dinner with us sometime," brings the equally agreeable and insincere answer, "Yes, I will." The insincerity is in the indefiniteness; "sometime" can often mean, "We are not expecting you," and its answer sometimes means, "Nor do I expect to go."

At the opposite extreme of these forms of insincerity are those who identify insult, boorishness, contempt, scorn, loud-mouthings with sincerity, candor and honesty. They boast that they are unafraid of public opinion or "what others think," or that they are always saying "what is best for you" or "what your best friends won't tell you." Little do they know that their readiness to criticize is a mask for their own egotism, afraid of having their own weakness pointed out, they keep others off guard by their poisoned attack.

The sincere are those who have an ensemble of virtues, who are equally good at speaking and listening; who have silences, as well as words; who are not opaque like curtains, but transparent like window panes. They speak, knowing that one day they will have to be judged by God and obliged to give "an account of every idle word." That makes them love the Truth and because they love it, they are always kind and charitable.

25. When Good People Do Wrong

The good sometimes do wrong. Let us face it. And when they do wrong it is not the same as the evil who do wrong. Evil is an exception in the life of the good; it cuts across the long road of their life as a tangent. But with the evil, good is an exception. A master pianist nay hit a wrong note, but everyone still knows him to be a good pianist. A beginner may hit a right note, but everyone knows that he is not a good player.

As a result the inner workings of the mind are quite different in the good doing wrong and the evil doing evil. In the latter, a hardening process sets in. Conscience first shouts; then, after repeated chokings it becomes so weak it can only whisper; finally, its voice is stifled altogether. Since such people willed to have no moral law except of their own making, God leaves them alone. It is terrible for the soul when God pursues it and drives it to perfection; but it is more terrible still when He leaves the soul to its own conceits.

The psychological effect is entirely different when those who truly love God do wrong. The difference between them and others is like to that between a waif who steals and a devoted son who steals. The first does not feel the rupture of a relationship; the second does. The latter has hurt one whom he really loves. Furthermore, the waif does not feel the urge to restore the broken buds of love, but the ordinary good boy does. There is a mysterious magnet operating in the case of the good. As the steel filings fly to the attraction of the magnet, leaving the dirt behind, so the good are pulled back again to God, but only after having shaken the dust of evil from their lives.

Picture two men married to two old shrews. One man was married before to a beautiful, wise, devoted wife who died. The other was never married before. Which of the two suffers the more? Obviously, the man who once knew love and happiness. So it is with doing evil. He who has known the inner peace of soul that comes from union with God undergoes greater agony and torture in his sin than the one who never was ushered into such treasures. The rich who become poor suffer more than the poor who never were rich. The soul which offends God Whom he loves suffers more than the soul who willed not to have God in his life.

This does not mean that the evil do not experience an agony. In the good, the effect of doing evil is moral and leads to repentance. In the evil, the effect is physical and psychological. It shows less in the soul and more in the mind and the body. The moral effect is sorrow, contrition, repentance, which leads to a restoration of fellowship with God and therefore peace. The physical or psychological effect is anxiety, fear, worry, psychoses and neuroses. The good take to their knees when they do wrong; the evil, if they have money enough, betake themselves to a couch. The good want their sins forgiven; the evil want them explained away. The good recover peace of soul; the evil have to be satisfied with peace of mind.

The explanation of this phenomenon is that the good have another principle of action in them than the evil. The evil are guided solely by the thought either of the satisfaction of the flesh or the spirit and that this world is all. But the good have another principle in them, entirely above nature, which is called grace, and by it they are united to God. This principle of grace is always rising up against their sin and generally triumphs over it with the slightest cooperation of the will. A man refrains from adultery because of the love he has for his wife. This principle of love militates against his carnal desires and, if he falls, pulls him back again to fidelity. So with grace. As St. Paul wrote to the pagan Romans: "I don't understand my own actions, because instead of doing what I want to do I do what I hate. Now if I don't want to do the very thing that I actually do, then I agree with the Law that it is, in fact, good" (Rm 7:15-16).

That is the point. The very regret one has is an admission that the law of God is right. A child told by his parents not to stick his finger in the fire does so. But he immediately discovers that their law was worthy of all honor.

There are two ways of knowing how good God is. One is never to lose Him, the other is to lose Him and find Him again.

26. Religion Not Popular

Almost everyone today wants religion, but everyone wants a religion that does not cost too much; that is why Christianity has been watered down to suit the modern mind. Everyone wants good health, but not everyone believes in dieting or giving up things which are bad for the body; in like manner, many have a vague aspiration for goodness without the will to implement it with sacrifice. The tens of thousands who in the past year have tried to give up smoking cigarettes, and then, after twenty-four hours, saw their resolution go up in smoke, can testify how little the modern mind is prepared for any kind of real sacrifice or self-denial.

It is not easy to say "No" to oneself; that is why so many philosophers have erected a philosophy of life based on saying "Yes" to every impulse and desire while dignifying it with the name " self-expression." But the fact still remains that serious progress in every walk of life demands some form of restraint, the doctor, the lawyer, the athlete, the singer, the businessman must all learn to "scorn delights and live laborious days" (John Milton, *Lycidas*, I, 64) if they are to attain their ideals. The expert in Oriental languages or archaeology cannot at the same time be a champion tennis player. In all walks of life, something must be sacrificed if something is to be gained; the mind is developed at the expense of the body, and the body at the expense of the mind.

Religion starts with an emptying of self. The Spirit cannot come into the soul until the ego begins to hang outside its tinsel dwelling the sign: "Immediate Occupancy." The ego or the selfish part of existence has to be broken like the shell of an egg before there can be the development of the personality which at the beginning is as helpless as a chick. But because the ego does not wish to be tamed and disciplined, it flatters itself that mortification is the "destruction of personality" and thus prepares for its own stagnation.

Detachment from certain things is essential for attachment to God, just as the attachment of a husband to a wife demands detachment from other women. As Thomas Aquinas said: "Man's heart adheres the more intensely to one thing, the more it is withdrawn from others." The human heart is like a stream which loses depth as it divides its waters of affection into many channels. A true patriot cannot serve several countries, and a truly religious person cannot serve both God and Mammon. Hence, our Lord gave the injunction: "Take up your cross daily and follow Me" (cf. Lk 9:23). First it is to be noted that the cross is personal. Most of us are willing to take up our own, or custom-built crosses — those that we have fitted to our own shoulders — but few there are who, like the Savior, are willing to take the cross that is handed to them.

It is the trials imposed upon us by others, such as their injustices, their harsh words, their knife-in-the-back attitudes, and their peevishness, that gall us; yet these are counted as the daily crosses of the man who would be truly religious. Much of the weariness of the spiritual life is due to the constant necessity of bearing the shortcomings of others, along with the never-ending strife against our own base inclinations. When other people begin "to get on our nerves," one must ask oneself if it is because they cross our moods or our wishes; in that case, it is self-will in us that adds to the weight of the cross.

Then begins the task of accepting such people as a cross, and through our patience and forgiveness, putting love where we do not find it. How many people there are in Church on Sunday sitting in the first seat of the pew, who resent anyone asking them to "please move over." They came to kneel before a cross, but they do not want one standing alongside them. How many there are too who sing lustily the hymn:

> *Were the whole realm of nature mine,*
> *That were an offering far too small,*

and then, when the collection box is passed, they drop in a nickel. The fact is religion is popular only when it ceases to be truly religious. Religion by its very nature is unpopular — certainly unpopular with the ego.

27. Wars and Rumors of Wars

There are two great evils in the world: sin and suffering. Sin is mortal, suffering is physical, and the latter is a result of the former. What happens to the body as pain, and to nature in the form of cyclones, earthquakes and floods, is ultimately an echo, a repercussion and effect of what has already happened in the moral universe. When the big wheel in a machine is cracked, all the little wheels get out of order. As we eliminate sin, we eliminate suffering; as we love God, we cease to hate others. And thus we engage in fewer wars.

The more morality and decency and virtue there are in the world, the more peace there will be in the world. Wars are consequences of a moral rebellion. The Scriptures boldly affirm that war is the result of egotism and selfishness. When civilization is made up of millions of men and women who are at war with themselves, it is not long until communities, classes, states and nations will be at war with one another. Every world war is a turbulent ocean made up of the confluent streams of millions of little wars inside the minds and hearts of unhappy people. War is the final logic of self-will.

War is not necessary, but it does become an inseparable ailment of any world that abandons the supremacy of the spirit. Nietzsche, after proclaiming the death of God in the nineteenth century, prophesied that the twentieth century would be a century of wars. There is a possible connection between the importance given to politics and the frequency of wars. In any era of history where politics is the major interest, war is the major consequence. This does not mean that one ought to subscribe to the dictum of Karl von Clausewitz that war is the prosecution of politics by other means. It does mean however, that since politics stresses expediency and pragmatism on a great scale that dedication to truth and morality are minimized. Since the latter are essential for peace, war becomes a greater possibility. When the people are interested in the raising of a family, the cultivation of virtues and the salvation of their souls, they act as a balance wheel against the power-motive of politics. But when both the state and the people give supremacy to politics, the stabilizing influence of society is lost, and with it come civil strife and discord and war.

There is much truth in the thesis of Pitirim Sorokin that as civilization in the modern sense of the term advances, there is an increase of war. There have always been more wars than peace. From 1496 B.C. to A.D. 1861 or in 3,358 years there were only 227 years of peace and 3,130 years of war; this makes 13 years of war for every year of peace. Within the last three centuries there have been 286 wars in Europe.

From 1500 B.C. to A.D. 1860 there were 8,000 treaties of peace which were supposed to remain in force forever. The average length of these treaties was two years. It is likely that there was never a single year when the world did not have a war at least in one country or the other. Two other analyses have revealed that, since the year 1100, England has spent half of its history fighting wars, France nearly half, and Russia three quarters.

It is not a very sweet pill for our civilized world to swallow, to realize that the false prophets of the last century who predicted an evolution of man into a god, and the necessary progress of humanity to a point where there would be no more war or disease or death, were wrong, and we are now living in a century of war. It behooves us all to admit that there is an evil tendency in our human nature, and that this tendency when uncontrolled by morality and grace will devolve more rapidly than it will evolve. It is our views of the human condition that have been wrong; by denying the possibility of sin and guilt, we have denied the very existence of perversity within us which makes war. Not all will sub-

mit to this moral regeneration through self-discipline, but those few who will, will be the leaven in
the mass of the world.

It is not our politics and our economics which
have to be changed first; it is we ourselves. It is the
wars within that have to be stopped. The remaking
of the world depends on the remaking of the individual. The return of the individual to God is the
condition of more peaceful times.

LEARNING

28. Pride and Humility

We can set ourselves above others, and feel superior to them in either of two ways: by our knowledge, or by our power; by flaunting what we know, or by using money and influence to make ourselves supreme. Such forms of behavior always spring from pride.

Now pride of the first kind — intellectual pride — changes its expression with the fashion of the age. In some periods of history (when the public idols were persons of learning, esteemed for their scholarship) the proud individual pretended to possess vast knowledge which was not really his. Intellectual bluffers were common. Phonies (who always wish to *seem*, rather than to *be*, whatever kind of leader is applauded in their age) put on a pretense of scholarship which was not theirs.

Such intellectual bluffers are less common today: we do not, in our society, reward our men of learning with sufficient glamor or publicity to make it worth the phoney's while to try to seem to be one of them. Traces of the old snobbery of the intellect still remain in those circles of the intelligentsia where the question, "Have your read such and such a book?" is used as a test of whether one is intellectually on his toes.

Nowadays the commoner form of intellectual

pride is negative. The proud do not exalt themselves; they tear the others down and thus accomplish the same goal in the end — that of finding themselves raised high above their fellows. The cynic and the scoffer are common examples of modern pride. They do not pretend to share the knowledge of the learned; they simply tell us that the scholar's knowledge is untrue, that the great disciplines of the mind are a tangle of outworn absurdities, that nothing is worth learning because everything is obsolete. The ignorant, boasting of their ignorance, thus try to establish themselves as superior to all those who know more than they: for they know what the others do not know — that study "is a waste of time."

The new-fashioned egotist of this type — those who scorn the knowledge others possess — are as guilty of pride as the old-fashioned intellectual snobs who pretended to wisdom they had not taken the trouble to absorb.

Both errors, the old and the new, might be rarer if education stressed, more than it does, the quality of receptivity. The child is humble before a fact; he loses himself in admiration of it. The older person, too often, asks of every fact, "How can I use this to extend my ego, to make a bigger splash among my fellows, to induce people to admire me more?" Ambition to *use* knowledge for our selfish ends drives out the humility which is required of us before we can learn anything.

Intellectual pride destroys the mood in which we learn; it also places a film of self over our eyes, so that we cannot enjoy the life around us. When we are preoccupied with ourselves we do not give our full attention to any person or thing that comes our way, and so we do not get, from each experience, the enjoyment it could give to us. It is because the small child knows that he is small, and accepts the fact without pretending to be big, that his world is a world of wonders. To every little boy, his father is a giant.

The capacity for wonder is killed in many universities. Students emerge interested in the question of whether they are at the top of the class, or the foot, or somewhere in the middle, working their way higher. This interest in the self and its rating poisons the proud person's life — for self-centeredness is always a form of pride.

The willingness to learn, to change, to grow is a quality of self-forgetfulness, of real humility.

It is the pride of the show-off which makes it impossible for him to learn — or, indeed, to teach the things he knows. For only the mind which humbles itself before the truth it wishes to impart can pass the knowledge on to other minds. The world has never known a humbler teacher than the Word of God Himself, who taught in simple parables and homely examples drawn from sheep and goats and lilies of the field, from patches on worn clothing and wine in new bottles.

Pride is a watchdog of the mind, which keeps out wisdom and the joy of life. Pride can reduce the whole vast universe to the compass of a single ego, self-contained, unwilling to expand.

29. The Obtrusiveness of Evil

One out of every seventeen persons in the United States suffers from some form of mental illness; one out of every two hospital beds is occupied by a mental patient; ten percent of the school children of New York were recently adjudged to be emotionally unstable. It was not that many years ago that H.G. Wells and others, in their false optimism, were telling us that in a short time we would be as gods, and that happiness would increase with economic prosperity. Religion, for the moment, was regarded as a kind of ambulance which took care of the sick until scientific progress could take over. Now alas, the beast who was evolving to become a god, has suddenly gone berserk before he has become a man.

A character in one of George Bernanos' novels asks, "Do you believe in hell, Pernichon?" The answer comes back, "Look, you need go no farther;

my house is a hell." Hell — which once was pictured "way down there" — is back again, but now "way in here" in the breast of man. He who was wont in saner days to confess his faults, admit personal guilt, and try to make some amends for both, is induced to become a kind of regurgitating sewer, vomiting the rottenness within; an analysis of the stagnant waters that comes from unconsciousness promises a cure, but it in most cases no more saves than an analysis of the waters of a sinking ship saves the vessel. The ancient principle of purgation of evil has now become a kind of curiosity in which a mind takes delight in its mental spewings after the fashion of the dog described in Sacred Scripture who "returns again to his vomit" (Pr 26:11).

Why the intense interest in crime? How explain it psychologically? It is a fact that more crimes are committed in one year on television than in six major cities of the United States; a threat or an act of violence is enacted every two and one half minutes on children's television shows. In the end, the police always catch up with the criminal, thus giving a smattering of justice. It is now a mark of a simpleton to exhibit a naive surprise at the quantity of evil that is in the world. This major interest in crime indicates something new — namely, the obtrusiveness of evil. Added to this is the psychological fact that evil is pictured in someone else. By depersonalizing it, by making it social and not personal, conscience is eased, at least for the moment. The Chinese have a proverb, "I thought that I was unfortunate because I had no shoes, until I saw a man who had no feet." By looking at the crime of others, we do get into a state of thinking that by comparison we cannot be so bad; aye! we may even be virtuous.

Modern man is naked. He has been stripped by false prophets who told him that his old clothes of morality were out of date. Now, none of the new suits he puts on can cover his nakedness — moreover, they give him considerable discomfort. The preoccupation with political evils has for the moment, as Dorothy Sayers points out, blinded us to the grosser sins of spiritual pride and intellectual sloth. But the obtrusiveness of evil is no reason for despair. Saner minds will see the issue more clearly. As our instability increases, it will be more clearly seen that if psychiatry is the final and absolute answer to the problem of evil — which no good psychiatrist would ever maintain — then no psychiatrist should ever be abnormal. He ought to be in civilization what the saint was in other days — its most stabilizing factor. We will also see bad economic conditions are not the cause of evil, otherwise no rich men would ever be cruel; sex license would no longer be held up as the cure, for if it were true, no unrepressed person would ever be tyrannical or a social problem. Within a short time, we will see that the source of evil is in the heart of each individual. When we begin to purge out what is wrong and turn to God for pardon, our mental health will surely return to us.

30. Entering into Oneself

Most of us know our neighbors better than we know ourselves. We can tell all their faults, enumerate all the scandals about them and even add a few for good measure, but we are hardly conscious of any single fault of our own. And yet the human being is the only creature in the universe who has the power of being able to look at himself in a mirror; to turn back on himself, judge his motives, see his faults and his good deeds, and thus either be pleased or angry with himself in the light of his conscience.

Most of us do not like to look inside ourselves for the same reason we do not like to open a letter that has bad news. Some try to get away from conscience by eliminating consciousness through alcoholism and drugs; others use the dubious technique of calling things by their wrong names, for example, calling darkness light, bitter sweet, and sweet bitter. Thus they seek to escape the eternal distinction of right and wrong. Speak of evil in its true terms and you rob it of half its seductiveness. "Sex" is less appealing when called "lust," "providing for the future" becomes vicious when labeled "avarice," and "asserting self" loses its glamor when called "egotism."

The great Greek historian, Lecky, said that the surest sign of utter degradation is when men speak of virtues as if they were vices, and of vices as if they were virtues. "They altered," he says, "the customary meaning of words in reference to actions. Men looked on deeds of infamy and were not shocked. The sin of the world and its moral corruption infected the air. Men were naked and not ashamed, not because they were innocent, but because no sense of guilt assailed them."

In our days when some politicians prostitute public office or else ally themselves with evil forces, they justify their wickedness on the ground that "they did nothing against the law." The only law for them becomes civil law, and their individual interpretation of it; never do they think of the moral law in their conscience, or the Ten Commandments. Even men who in their own personal lives are moral will nevertheless condone and even approve anything their party does even when manifestly dishonest or immoral. It is for such subservience to the trivialities of petty parties that the number of true patriots in public office steadily declines, leaving the real patriots to the battlefields.

This paralysis of conscience reaches its final stage in the mind when, as pure water becomes loathsome to the drunkard, so does justice and virtue to the depraved conscience. Then comes that mentality spoken of by the Roman satirist: "*Virtutem videant, intabescantque relicta.*" "Let them see virtue and pine for it, for now it is beyond their reach." No condition of the mind is worse than to forget the heavens from which we fall, for then we lose all aspirations for conversion.

This condition of a moral awakening is the same for all men as it was for the prodigal son who "entered into himself" (Lk 15:17). Most people do not consider the state of their conscience until they are driven inside by the collapse of everything on the outside. As poverty, famine and disillusionment made the prodigal "come to himself," so it may be that some great catastrophe may be a necessary curtain raiser to a spiritual regeneration.

The earliest summons of a conscience is generally met with rebellion and resistance. Those who hate religion do so because of the evil in their life. When conscience begins to awaken, it exasperates into a more vicious rebellion. We become moral Laocoons, stung into a living martyrdom with the sting of the serpents of our guilt which lie in the bosom of our conscience. When remorse scourges us, the old ego becomes mad and even more violent than ever before. Temper flares, hatred of others multiplies as a projection of a disguised hatred of self, and a despondency seizes the soul from which no distraction gives relief. But all these violent outbursts against virtue are really nothing but the gathering of dark and angry clouds which one day will be dissolved in showers.

Those who have to counsel other people should therefore never take too seriously the seeming wrath against goodness and morality. It may be only the swathing grave cloths out of which the new person is to rise. The individual really does not hate goodness, but himself. But in his pride he will not admit it, until at last restlessness and uneasiness drive him to his knees for pardon and for light. When he begins to blame himself and not economic conditions, or his companions, or his grandmother, or his ductless glands, he finds the key to happiness. There was more than fable in the old mythology which told of Pandora's box — a veritable receptacle of ills made tolerable only because there was hope at the bottom. Modern man is not coming to God from the goodness in the world; he is coming to God from the evil in his own heart.

31. Reading

Within the past year non-fiction books surpassed in sales fiction or novels. This is a happy trend in our contemporary civilization, for the reader of a serious book must always keep an active mind, whereas the reader of fiction may be passive and accept the doings and the musings of the characters as they are unfolded. It is interesting to make a comparison of the book reviews in the London Times Literary Supplement and the book reviews in many of our leading newspapers. Just for the fun of it, we counted the number of novels reviewed in one of the book review sections of an American newspaper, and found 25 were reviewed in one issue, counting as non-fiction everything that was not a novel, there were only 13 serious books reviewed. Turning to the London Times Literary Supplement, we counted 9 novels reviewed, as compared with 40 works of non-fiction. The novel has value and oft times can present a moral or economic problem in the concrete far better than can be done in the abstract writing of non-fiction.

While each person is entitled to his preferences, the fact still remains that for the complete development of the mind, there must be serious and intelligent reading — not just reading. A king of Poland in the eighteenth century, speaking of those

who read too much and absorbed too little, re-
flected: "A well-read fool is the most pestilent of
blockheads; his learning is a flail which he knows
not how to handle, and with which he breaks his
neighbor's shins as well as his own." As the stomach can suffer from indigestion, so can the mind. If
too many ideas are poured into it and there are not
sufficient juices of the intellect to absorb them, a
queer kind of literary constipation follows. As Milton
said, one can be "deep versed in books and shallow
in himself."

Not long ago, we were talking to a young college student who boasted of his vast reading, and
said that Freud developed the idea of the inferiority complex. When it was suggested that possibly
he was confusing Freud with Adler, his remark was:
"Well, I ought to know, I visited Vienna and that is
where Freud lived." Many people live under the illusion that they have read more than they actually
have. There is hardly anyone who has been through
college who does not live under the false belief that
he has read Darwin's *Origin of Species* or Spenser's
Faery Queen. It has been said that some of the great
geniuses of the past never read half as much as the
mediocre geniuses today, but what they read they
understood and incorporated into a much deeper
dimension of knowledge.

There is a world of difference between a mind
that has in it ten thousand bits of uncorrelated in-

formation, and a mind that is like an organism in which one fact or truth is functionally related to every other truth, as the heart is related to the legs and arms. The wisest of men reads out of a philosophy of life, as he eats out of a philosophy of health. Mental garbage is as scrupulously avoided by the eyes in reading, as another kind of garbage is avoided by the lips. On the other hand, certain "hard" reading, such as Plato, Aquinas, Toynbee pass like iron in the blood and into the mind, giving it consistency and strength.

The easiness with which reading matter can be procured today has much to do with the ministering to lower tastes. Those who had a taste for philosophy in the days of Aristotle, a yearning for poetry in the days of Dante, for metaphysics in the days of Abelard, and for sacred science when the monasteries held all the treasures of knowledge, spared no effort to absorb learning. But now that reading is accessible in every drugstore and city corner, the discrimination has decreased with the availability.

After a time, useless reading weakens the mind rather than strengthens it; then reading becomes an excuse for the mind to lie dormant while thoughts are poured over it like chocolate over ice cream. The mind is like an hourglass through which ideas pass like sands, nothing remaining. We, in the modern age, have more leisure than those of a century ago, but we know less what to do with it. Our education is rightly preparing us to make a living. But let education not forget that since we have more leisure than working hours, it might do well to teach us how to spend our leisure. Give a person a taste for the intellectual, the spiritual and the moral, and you make them happy. As a Latin poet put it: *"Emollit mores, nec sinit esse feros."* Reading civilizes conduct and keeps it from becoming barbarous.

32. Goodness in Others

There are three different ways in which we may judge others: with our passions, our reason, and our faith. Our passions induce us to love those who love us; our reason makes us love all people within certain limits; our faith makes us love everyone, including those who do us harm and who are our enemies. The greatest drama in life takes place when the other person is wrong from our point of view. Almost every quarrel has its basis in a mutual misunderstanding. Each of us is really an open book, but some who know us do not read the book well. We speak with great sympathy of those who understand us or who read us aright, and with some diffidence of those who do not understand.

Perhaps no one understands us better than saints, not only because they correct their bad judgment of us through their own weakness, but also because they see us as souls precious in the sight of God. St. Francis de Sales used to say: "O the beautiful souls of sinners." It was not their sins he loved, but their souls. The Curé of Ars used to walk two or three blocks alongside his country church where there was a long line of penitents waiting to see him. He would pick out the great sinners and reserve for them the greatest sympathy. When one is in trouble, one should never go for advice to one who never says prayers or who has not passed through suffering.

There is much more goodness in most people than shows on the surface. Underneath the dross of every human there is some gold. When the sinful woman came into Simon's house, he continued to regard her as a sinner even after she had repented. He would not give anyone a chance to be different. It was no wonder the Divine Savior had to say to Simon: "Do you see this woman?" (Lk 7:44) Simon did not see her as she was, but only as he wanted to think of her. He thought he knew all the facts, but as one of the professors of the College of France once said to his students: "Seek the facts above all else, but remember that the facts can be wrong." What he meant was that false conclusions are too often drawn from the facts, and particularly about people.

The good are not always good in all things, and the wicked are not always wicked in all things. As it has been said, "There is so much good in the worst of us and so much bad in the best of us," that it ill behooves any of us to talk about the rest of us. We often carry our faults in sacks behind our backs and the faults of our neighbors in open baskets in front of us. The separation of people into sheep and goats will take place only at the last day. Until then we are forbidden to make any classification. It is very likely that there will be many surprises in heaven. Many people will be there that we never expected to find, and many will not be there whom we expected to see; and finally, we probably will be most surprised to find ourselves there.

Our Divine Lord said: "Judge not and you will not be judged" (Mt 7:1). By the mere fact that we judge someone else, we have already judged ourselves. How do some women know that other women are catty, unless they themselves know how it feels to be catty. The evil that is said of others is often because one is jealous of what they have. Some believe that the good qualities of others have been stolen from them. Jealousy is the tribute which mediocrity pays to genius.

One day in a group of girls, there was much admiration expressed for the dimples in the cheek of one of them. But another of them said sneeringly:

"Weak face muscles." She felt that to praise another meant to condemn her.

A good rule to follow is always to judge the neighbor by his best moments rather than by his worst; not to call him a poor piano player because he hits one poor note in an entire evening, but to judge him because of all the right notes he hit. Nothing so much encourages a merciful judgment of others as the Divine warning that as we judge others, so shall we be judged. As we show mercy, we shall receive mercy. We harvest what we sow. Most people demand of their neighbor much more than God demands of them. God is more merciful to the men who mock Him than men are merciful to the gods they make. When David sinned, God gave him the choice of being punished either by Him or by man. David chose God — His Mercy is greater.

33. The Right Drive for Superiority

The most common judgment passed today on others is: "Oh, he has an inferiority complex." It would be much truer to say of those really so complicated that they have a superiority complex, that is an unjustified drive toward superiority. But even here, it is well to remember that there is a right and wrong kind of superiority. The wrong kind of superiority is domination over others, boastfulness, egotism, self-will and cruelty. The right kind of superiority is striving for self-perfection in the moral order.

Our Blessed Lord suggested that we be satisfied with nothing less than perfection: "So *you* be perfect as your Heavenly Father is perfect" (Mt 5:48). This does not mean that we are to be perfect as God is perfect, but to be perfect in a God-like and not a human way. What is startling about this command is that we are bidden not to imitate others, but God. The Divine Master would produce not character, but a better character. To Him, it is not great virtue to love those who love us. If such be the case, He asks: "If you love those who love you, what reward will you have? Don't the tax collectors also do the same?" (Mt 5:46). Virtue to Him was not democratic, but aristocratic; it was high above the mass-level, not one that struck the happy medium between the good and the bad. The crux of virtue is not on the number of those who practice it, but in its principles. "Everybody is doing it" may determine democratic practices, but it is not character or virtue.

"What are you doing more than others?" — that is the acid test. He who thinks he has done enough has done nothing. The regularities of constitutional goodness, the observance of common decencies, politeness, generosity, good cheer, the good affections which nature prompts — these are the perfection of the average person, not of God. There are few who would not claim to some moral distinction if they were honest, and paid their income taxes, gave to the poor, and allowed others their point of view. But it appears that even when we have done these things, we may still be asked by the standard of Divine Superiority: "What are you doing more than others?"

It is common today to identify a Christian with a gentleman, or a "nice person." Certainly we should strive to have a world in which there are as many nice people as possible, such as those who give their seats to ladies in subways, who speak with appreciation of the United Nations, who help old women across the street and are kind to the deaf. But we must not make the mistake of believing that by that fact they have become Christian. As a Professor of Philosophy at Cambridge said recently in a television address: "A world of nice people, content in their own goodness, niceness, looking no further, turned away from God, would be just as much in need of salvation as a miserable world — and might even be more difficult to save."

The superiority for which men strive today is generally economic or social, not spiritual or moral. When one hears of those who leave the mass-level and dedicate themselves to spiritual perfection, the tendency is to argue: (1) There is nothing in it but an "escape." (2) Those who pretend to see something in it are posing. (3) I hate them for it. The reason there is a hatred is because these people in the end may be having something that I do not have.

No personality is adequately expressed on the average level. The average person from a moral point of view is common. He who tries to keep on the level with others has already condemned himself to failure. The development of a spiritual personality is in going the extra mile and challenging conventional morality. "If someone forces you to go one mile," said Our Lord, "go with him two" of your own accord (Mt 5:41). The weakness of our age is in want of great men and women. It is hard to resist the current. Someone must completely detach himself from the ordinary run of politicians if he is to save politics; economists must break with the ordinary run of the mill of capital and labor commonplaces, if economics is to be saved. In other words, we need saints. These are not easy to make. First of all — because we do not always want the best; the best demands sacrifice of the ordinary and the discipline of the lower self. God, in His turn, finds it hard to give, because He gives only the best — moral perfection — and few there are who want it. As Augustine said at one point in his life, "I want to be good, dear Lord… but not now — a little later on."

34. Age

As medical science increases life expectancy it has also brought to the fore the problem of growing old. The average age when life's lease runs out is, in France 61 years, in Sweden 65, in the low Countries 68, in the United States 64 and in India 27.

Cicero wrote on old age and enumerated several of its advantages. Horace spoke of the elders as "praisers of things that are past" (Epistles, Bk. III, *Ars Poetica*, I. 173). St. Peter in his Pentecost Sermon said the "young men will see visions, and the old men will dream dreams" (Ac 2:17). Youth is full of hope and sees visions in the future; age is retrospect and recalls the glories of the past. Our Blessed Lord told Peter that old age is a restriction of liberty: "But when you are old, you will stretch out your hands and another will bind you and lead you where you do not wish to go" (Jn 21:18).

Each age has its compensations and also a particular vice against which it must battle. Youth has to struggle against the uncontrolled impulses of the flesh. As dirt is matter in the wrong place, so lust is flesh in the wrong place. In middle age, the passion that has to be watched is egotism or the unbridled craving for power. Here the unregulated impulse moves from the flesh to the mind, from sex to selfishness, from carnality to pride. In the third stage of life, the tendency to avarice supplants the other two. Here it is not what is within a person, namely his body or his mind which distracts him, but what is outside him — the world, riches and possessions. As if conscious of his life passing he would give a security to his mortality by filling up his barns even to the night the angel requires his soul of him (cf. Lk 12:20).

Where there is a sense of dependence on God, a consciousness that this life is a stewardship, and a firm conviction that what we do here determines our eternity, old age does not bring sorrow or regret, but rather a joy as it did to Simeon (cf. Lk 2:29). But where life is empty there are several dangers, the first of which is alcoholism. The medical profession today is alarmed at those who have passed middle age who would dull with stimulants the little of life that still remains. The cause is very often both moral and physical. It is moral when the attempt to drown either an unrequited sense of guilt or else escape responsibility for the emptiness of their lives. It is physical when they try to excite new strength to compensate for what they know is passing, or else give themselves an illusory world with its false sense of power. St. Paul had this in mind when he said: "Urge the older men to be sober" (Tt 2:2).

Modern civilization has little respect for the aged for the same reason it has little for tradition. There is a love for the antique but not for the ancient. Yet the aged are to culture what memory is to the mind. Just as one cannot think without going into the storehouse of memory for the foundation stones of thought, so neither can a civilization progress without its memory which is tradition. The ancients surrounded their elders with great respect. The Greek word "*presbus*" was used not only to indicate an old man, but also an important and respectable ambassador chosen because of his experience. From this word has also come not only the word "*presbyter*" or "priest" but also "*presbyope*" which indicates one who is farsighted rather than nearsighted —which is one of the qualities associated with old age.

Those who have a philosophy of life are not troubled with age. Our last days should be the best days. The evening praises the day; the last scene commands the act; and the music reserves its sweetest strains for the end. Simeon, when he saw the Divine Babe, sang: "Now You can dismiss Your servant, O Lord in peace" (Lk 2:29). He speaks like a merchant who has got all his goods on shipboard, and now desires the master of the ship to hoist sail and be homeward bound.

Happy old age which uses this life to purchase the next has an outer and an inner contentment. The outward work is the spreading of charity, the using of experience to help others. The hard work is the rounding of the soul into as great a perfection as possible to meet its God.

The secret of growing old is in this counsel an old man once gave a youth: "Repent on your last day." But the youth answered: "But who knows when my last day will be?" For that reason said the Saint: "Repent today for it would be tomorrow."

35. Self-Inflation

One of the celebrated portrait artists of the world once said that he never knew a person to sit for a portrait who did not constantly talk about himself. This may be explained psychologically as a desire to impress the artist with his greatness, in order that the artist might translate it onto the canvas. But it is more likely that the habit of egotism was already so deeply encrusted that self-praise was rather automatic, it showed itself in the Pullman car as well as in the studio. Rich men perhaps more than others are the greatest boasters, though it may be unconscious. Confusing *having* with *being* they think that since they possess material greatness, therefore, they must necessarily be great. Such proud people are much more subject to worry and anxiety than those who are not proud, for every little trial registers very sharply through their morbidly sensitive skin.

Nothing has so much contributed to egotism, pride, conceit, swell-headedness and braggadocio, as the assumption that an "inferiority complex" is always wrong. If the failure to assert oneself, to push others aside in seeking first places at table, is the mark of a psychic disease, then satanic pride is on the throne. Depreciation of the efforts of others, the swaggering playing out of a dream and an illusion, an excessive tenderness about any personal insults and a callousness toward the feeling of others become the daily behavior pattern.

The egotist, standing alone in his self-imagined greatness, lives in a world of lie, because the truth about himself would puncture his self-inflation. Pride rightly has been called the source of all other evils. As the great poet put it "Fling away ambition; By that sin fell the angels; How can man then, the image of his Maker, expect to win by it?" (Shakespeare, *Henry the Eighth*, Act III, Scene ii, Line 441).

A word hardly ever mentioned in modern speech is "Humility" or the virtue which regulates a person's undue estimation of himself. Humility is not underestimating oneself, such as a talented singer denying that he can sing. Humility is truth, or seeing ourselves as we really are — not as we think we are, not as the public believe us to be, or as our press notices describe us. If the candle compares itself with the lightning bug, it boasts of the greater light; but if it compares itself with the sun, it sees itself but as its feeble ray. As the artist must judge his painting by the sitter, as the die maker must judge his coin by the model, so we must judge ourself by our Maker and all that He intended us to be.

The humble are not cast down by the censures or the slights of others. If they have unconsciously given occasion for them, they amend their faults; if they deserve them not, they treat them as trifles Humility also prevents putting an extravagant value on distinctions and honors. Praise will generally make the humble person uncomfortable, because he knows that whatever talents he has are gifts from God. He receives praise as the window receives light, not as the battery receives a current. The humble may be great, but if they possess that virtue, they hire no press agents, they blow no trumpets, they affect no mannerisms, they unfold no banners, they court no adulation, but while aiding and enlightening others, they long to be like the angels who, while ministering to others, are themselves unseen.

Humility is the pathway to knowledge. No scientist would ever learn the secrets of the atom if, in his conceit, he told the atom what he thought it ought to do. Knowledge comes only with humility before the object which can bring us truth.

In like manner, many minds today will not accept Revelation or faith because their pride has blocked the inflow of new knowledge. Only docile minds can receive new truth. Pride makes a person insoluble and, therefore, prevents his entering into amalgamation with others. Humility, on the contrary, because of its basic receptivity to the good of others, makes it possible to receive the joys of union with God. That is why Our Divine Lord suggested that university professors will have to become children to enter the kingdom of heaven; they must admit, like children, that God knows more than they do.

36. Truth — Forgotten Ideal

Submission is one of the deepest needs of the human heart. After a century and a half of false liberalism, in which it was denied that anything is true, and that it makes no difference what you believe, the world reacted to totalitarianism. It grew tired of its freedom, just as children in progressive schools grow tired of their license to do whatever they please. Freedom fatigues those who want to shirk responsibility. Then it is they look for some false god into whose hands they can throw themselves, so they will never have to think or make decisions for themselves. Nazism, Fascism, and Communism came into being during the twentieth century, as a reaction against false liberalism.

Self-will always repudiates a truth which challenges it. However successful self-will may be, it is never satisfied; that is why the egotist is always critical. The "head that wears the crown is uneasy," not because he is tired of the crown, but because he is tired of himself. He has it within his power to do anything he pleases, and this living without boundaries and limitations becomes as dull and stagnant as a swamp. A river must be happier than a swamp because it has banks and boundaries; a swamp is a valley of liberty that lost its shores and became "liberal."

The only ones who are really free from the bondage and the burden of self are those who hold to a truth. "The truth will make you free," said Our Divine Lord (Jn 8:32). Only the boxer who knows the truth about fighting is free to stay on his feet. Only the one who knows the truths of engineering is free to build a bridge that will stand. The lover of truth is under an eternal law of rectitude; as he submits to it, he enjoys peace. Truth is not something that we invent; if we do, it is a lie; rather truth is something we discover, like love. In that great book of C.S. Lewis called *Screwtape Letters*, there is a series of correspondence between an uncle devil in hell and a young nephew devil on earth. The young devil is trying to win souls over to himself by talking about the "Truth of Materialism." The old devil reprimands him saying that he must not talk about "truth"; that is the word that is used by our "enemy, God." You might confuse minds; get them to inquire whether a thing is "liberal or reactionary," "right or left," "modern or behind the times." Evidently Screwtape, the old devil, has succeeded pretty well with politicians and others.

Truth does not challenge, but truth does develop. Two and two do not make four in the thirteenth century, and sixteen in the twentieth, but arithmetic does develop into geometry, and geometry into calculus. Nor is truth easy to discover, particularly when it affects our lives. There are two kinds of truth; speculative and practical. Speculative truth is the truth of knowing, such as comes to us from philosophy, mechanics, physics and chemistry. Practical truth, however, is concerned with doing and living, such as ethics and morals.

The first kind of truth is very easy to accept, e.g., London is the capital of England. The reason is because it does not in any way involve a change in our conduct. It makes no practical difference to our lives. But the truth of morality, such as purity, justice and prudence and charity arc not so easy for acceptance, because they often demand a revolution in our behavior. That is why men are more willing to accept objections against a principle of morality than against a theory of science. Our Divine Lord referred to the difficulty of accepting practical truths when He said: "You will not come to me because your lives are evil" (cf. Jn 5:19-47).

Truth is a narrow path; either side is an abyss. It is easy to fall either to the right or to the left; it was easy to be an idealist in the nineteenth century, as it is easy to be a materialist in the twentieth century; but to avoid both abysses and walk that narrow path of truth is as thrilling as a romance. Truth is like the veins of metal in the earth; it is often very thin and runs not in a continuous layer. If we lose it once, we may have to dig for miles to find it again. Grains of truth are like grains of gold that prospectors find; they can be discovered after a long search; they must be sifted from error with great patience; they must be buried with sacrifice to erase the dross and washed in the streams of honesty. Notice how often today men in public life accuse one another of "lying." Why is it they never speak of truth? May it not be that they studied in the same school as Pilate and asked "What is Truth?" (Jn 18:38) and then turn their backs on it. It takes a heap of virtuous living for any one of us to discover Truth.

37. The Need of Memory

The experiences of the past are recorded in memory, which is made up of thousands of yesterdays. The older one gets, the more store we set by it. The young look forward, but the old look backward. There is a kind of impatience about the present, due principally to the innate yearning in the human soul for immortality, and for joys that do not fade and treasures that do not corrupt. Many a person recalls his school days and wishes that he had studied harder or else had stayed longer in school. Americans who go to Paris with their one year of book-French become slightly provoked because the horses and dogs understand some French and they do not. Usually they try to make up for it by shouting in English to the French. It reminds one of the preacher whose notes were found on the pulpit on Monday morning by the janitor. The latter was very amused to find this written in the margin: "Argument weak. Shout like the deuce!"

Today there seems to be a conspiracy against the noble faculty of memory. This conspiracy stems from two quarters generally: poor educational theory and bad medical practice. Education today practically ignores memory. Dr. Hutchins says that 50% of the male population of Chicago are functionally illiterate; by this he means they can read, but they cannot tell you what it means. Memory is neglected in almost all educational practice today. This neglect is in part due to the general repudiation of tradition, which should characterize every advance in culture. We in the modern world are alienating ourselves from the past under the false assumption that nothing that was ever thought before or done before is worth preserving.

Children are hardly ever asked to memorize anything. Spelling is, as a result, conspicuously weak in the rising generation. Students are told that it is not so important to know anything; it is only important to know where to find it. The trouble with this idea is that you often need things at once. One knows that money is in the bank, but it does little good to know that, when you want to buy a paper. Health may be found at certain resorts, but it is well to possess it independently of travel catalogues. In a former generation, the students learned by heart many of the soliloquies of Shakespeare, the great battles of history and the line of English Kings during the flowering of English literature. But Pragmatism and Marxism ignore the memory of the human race, either because the only thing that matters is the useful, or because the good of former times is regarded as anti-revolutionary.

Not trained in memorizing either facts or ideas, it is now almost impossible for many to make an announcement on the radio or television without reading from notes. Everyone remembers the Fourth of July orator who tried to talk without any notes, until he said that we all ought to be grateful to the "One from Whom our rights and liberties descended." He reached into his pocket, pulled out his notes and then added: "Almighty God."

The other attack on memory comes from that small group of practitioners who believe the way to treat the melancholy, the worries and frustrations of people is to give them sleeping tablets, so they will not remember. This only covers over the ulcerous part while rank corruption undermines all within.

Memory is the autobiography of our lives, and though we cover the pages with barbiturates, the indelible record remains. Since it survives with unhappy memories, the solution is not to drug it, but to face it. Since memory contains the material on which our conscience passes judgment, it follows that the best way to rid ourselves of bad memory is to cleanse consciences. Then the record which was once a shame begins to be our glory. Since it is a fact that the more displeasing certain things are, the more apt they are to be recalled, may not this be an evidence of the mercy of God, Who shows us the wound, that we can call Him in as Physician of our souls?

WISDOM

38. Stick Out Your Tongue

Ours is the most talkative age in history, not only because we can multiply words a million fold through radio, television, recordings and print, but also because there are few who like to be listeners. Even youth is called upon to give its views before it has had time to learn principles. If you just put your head between your hands today to think out some thing, you are asked if you have a headache. What we say is a revelation of the heart.

Scripture says: "From the abundance of the heart the mouth speaks" (Mt 12:34). Modern psychology has just begun to discover that what is in the heart sooner or later makes its report on the tongue. Socrates well said: "Speak that I may see thee." When a doctor would ascertain the condition of the health of his patient, he says: "Stick out your tongue." As on that member is registered to a great extent the physical state, so also is registered there the moral condition. If there is a skunk in the cellar it will not be long until it makes itself known in every room in the house. If jealousy, hate, evil and resentment are in the heart, it will not be long until they find utterance on the tongue.

Science tell us that the vibrations of speech are recorded through the centuries. Some have even spoken of the possibility of picking up in the universe the great voices of the past, even that of the Word Himself. The spoken word is like the spent arrow; it cannot be recalled in its flight but its responsibilities endure forever. Alpine climbers bid travelers at certain points not to shout too loudly, lest the vibrations of the voice precipitate a terrible avalanche. The hasty or intemperate word, or the whispered slander has often provoked great crises in history which have drowned thousands in their misery.

It is interesting how through history law has recognized the dangers of the unbridled tongue. In China, excessive talkativeness on the part of a woman was regarded as sufficient grounds for putting her away. Manu, the legislator of the Hindus, wrote "Whatever glances are reserved for the slayer of a priest or the murderer of a woman or child are reserved for those who give false evidence." Augustus Caesar ordered that the authors of all libels were to be punished by death. The art of speech has been studied with great competency from Aristotle onward, but few there are who regard the morals of speech. If a moral person sat down to decide the one secular profession he or she would approach with the greatest reluctance, because of the responsibility it involved, that profession would be the publishing of a newspaper. An unskilled doctor could kill the body, but the person who would use the printed word either to kill a soul, or deprive it of a single grain of divine truth, or put into a single germ of evil would be guilty of the greater crime.

As Christ is the Word Incarnate, so every spoken word is the thought incarnate. As Hawthorne said: "Nothing is more unaccountable than the spell that often lurks in the spoken word."

A kind word gives encouragement to the despondent heart, and a cruel word makes others sob their way to the grave. There are not sufficient apostles of encouragement in the world today. The great tragedy is that so many people are unloved in the right sort of way. Instead of trying to find out what is worst in people, everyone would be happier if there were a search for even just one good point.

Street-cleaners were one day discussing a companion who had died and who indeed had few good points. But one stood up for him, scraped the bottom of the barrel for something good to say about him, and came up with the praise: "But whatever you say about him, he did sweep well around the corners." There is good in everything if we but distill it out.

39. The Sensitiveness of the Innocent

Society can live only by standards of right and wrong. But these standards can be lost. In earlier days, men knew why anything was right or wrong; they could give reasons to deter members of society from acting in a certain way. But, curiously enough, our age has forgotten the reasons. Right and wrong are largely matters of "feeling," and even when something is said to be "wrong in itself," such as murder, few seem to be able to say why it is wrong. Morality is thus reduced to something as personal as taste; the mind becomes like the stomach, preferring right to wrong as it might choose pickles rather than choose cucumbers: "It all depends upon your point of view."

The ancient Greek historian Thucydides, in speaking of the class struggle to which his society had degenerated, observed: "The meaning of words has no longer the same relation to things, but was changed by them as they thought proper. Reckless daring was held to be loyal courage; prudent delay was the excuse of a coward; moderation was the disguise of unmanly weakness, frantic energy was the true quality of a man. The conspirator who wanted to be safe was a recreant in disguise; the lover of violence was always trusted and his opponent was suspected" (*History of the Peloponnesian Wars*).

The false principles behind this "feeling" theory of right and wrong are very evident: first, it is held that every experience is for its own sake, whether that experience be sexual, political, social, or economic. The experience cannot be for the sake of anything else, there being nothing else but the self. Second, if we attempt to make any judgment on our experience, it must be done solely on the basis of whether or not the experience is pleasurable to the ego; if it makes me "feel good" it is right. Finally, since pleasure or thrill or utility is the sole standard of judgment, it follows the more intense the thrill, the more useful anything is to the self, the better it is.

In contrast with this position, compare what might be called the sensitiveness of innocence. The sensitiveness of innocence does not mean ignorance or "not having lived." Rather it is an awareness of what is good and true because one has avoided the false and the evil. The grammarian, who knows good style, is very sensitive to errors in writing or speaking; the physician is sensitive to disease and any deviation from the norm of health; the philosopher can detect at once a false reasoning process, the director of any orchestra, despite the number of musicians he has before him, can hear the false note from the smallest and least important of the instruments. So in the moral order, when Divine Innocence sat at table with a traitor, he said: "One of you is about to betray Me" (Jn 13:21). Holiness can quickly detect blots.

The instinctive reaction of good children to evil is not due to their rational immaturity, but to their maturity in innocence. Such judgments of innocence and purity are totally different from suspicion. Suspicion can often be a reflection of one's own failings. "Judge not and you will not be judged" (Mt 7:1). Often, the sins we most loudly condemn in others are those to which we are most secretly attached, or else constitute our greatest weakness. Purity is never suspicious but looks for some ground for reposing trust. It has a power of apprehension, a penetration, an insight, a talent for psychological discovery that comes not to those who have been infected by wrong. How often the judgment of a child in a family about a visitor is more correct than the judgment of the parents. Innocence made them detect a blemish which the less innocent failed to see. Grown-ups who have surrendered even the quest of goodness are often fearful of the innocence of children, not because they fear to contaminate them, but because they feel condemned unconsciously by the innocent. At the Last Supper when the Savior said that "one" was about to betray Him, "all" asked: "Is it I?" No one can be sure of his goodness before innocence.

A society that needs healing and regeneration will receive it mostly from the innocent. The pure can look on the impure without contempt. It was Divine Innocence Who asked of a sinful woman: "Where are they who accused you?" (Jn 8:10). There was no condemnation in Him Who was Righteous-

ness itself; so there are sympathy and forgiveness
and healing in the wings of the innocent.

40. Patience

The opposite of "flying off the handle" is *patience* —
another virtue forgotten by our modern world, although Our Blessed Lord said: "By your patience
you will save your souls" (Lk 21:19). The Greek
origin of the word *patience* suggests two ideas: one
continuance, the other submission. Combined, they
mean submissive waiting, a frame of mind which is
willing to wait because it knows it thus serves God
and His Holy purposes. A person who believes in
nothing beyond this world is very impatient, because he has only a limited time in which to satisfy
his many wants. The more materialistic a civilization is, the more it is in a hurry. Douglas Woodruff,
the English essayist, said that "Americans do not like
Rome; they heard it was not built in a day." The
Chinese, on the other hand, can wait for centuries,
for their wants are not compassed in a generation.

Patience is not something one is born with, it
is something that is achieved, such as seeing. A baby
has to learn to see — to distinguish objects, and to
learn distances. Sight is a gift of nature, but seeing

has to be won. When Our Lord healed the blind man, he had to learn how to see, for he said that to him "men looked like trees walking" (Mk 8:24). So it is with self-possession and patience, but such a virtue is developed by resistance and control. The big problem all of us have to face is whether we will, under difficulties, ride out the storm to port. Of course, if we do not know *why* we are living, then we must substitute tiny little wishes for one great consuming purpose; and this makes life miserable and unhappy.

To us, often, the principal thing is the frustration, the war, the dislocation, the chaos, and the confusion. But patience ought to be the guiding virtue of the soul in the midst of this "confusion worse confounded." The winning of the battle of life is nothing but the winning of our souls, and souls are won by patience under tribulation.

Patience is not a virtue to be practiced only by the sick and by those in prison. Actually, few virtues are more essential for peace of soul, for there are hardly any circumstances of life where it cannot be practiced. There are four great areas of life in which patience can be learned. *First*, in the midst of provocations, that is, the indifference of others, the incivility and haughtiness of those with whom we work, the vexations at home, in the office, and on the highway. One of the reasons why people who are calm at home are impatient behind the steering wheel is because they know, as they shout at other drivers, that they are unknown. They regard anonymity as a shield for their character. *Second*, in disappointments; the rain on the day of the picnic, the late dinner guest, the cancelled visit, and the honor that never came through test us. Giving way to violence under these circumstances is a loss of self-possession. *Third*, restraints. No one can always be his or her own master. The tin can that will not open, the key that will not turn, the zipper that refuses to zip — all these are circumstances under which losing one's temper is to lose inner calm. It does no good to blame the club when the golfer is at fault. To be impatient is to aggravate the evils we must endure, and thus postpone their solution. *Fourth*, injuries and wrongs. No station is so high as to be immune from unjust criticism. The higher we climb, the better the target we make for sticks and stones! It is well to remember under such circumstances what Walter Winchell once said: "No man will ever get ahead of you as long as he is kicking you in the seat of your pants."

There are many who excuse themselves, saying that if they were in other circumstances they would be much more patient. This is a grave mistake, for it assumes that virtue is a matter of geography, and not of moral effort. It makes little difference where we are; it all depends on what we are thinking about. What happens to us is not so important, but rather how we react to what happens. Judas and Peter both sinned against the Lord, and He called them both devils. But one became a Saint, because he overcame his weakness with the help of God's grace.

It is the winds and the winters which try the herbs, the flowers, and the trees, and only the strongest survive. So tribulation tries the soul, and in the strong it develops patience, and patience, in its turn, hope, and hope finally begets love.

Patience is the great remedy against becoming panicky. To be able to use reason and good judgment when everyone else goes to pieces not only saves self, but also neighbor. Men use reason better when they are calm, women use reason best at the point where man loses it. Passion impairs reason in a man; in a woman it does not. But, regardless of these differences, the patient soul can use judgment and counsel when all others are agitated and disturbed. Patience is power. As an Eastern proverb put it: "With time and patience the mulberry leaf becomes satin." Patience is not absence of action; rather it is "timing"; it waits on the right time to act, for the right principles and in the right way. The yoke sits easiest on the neck of the patient ox, and he feels his chain the lightest who does not drag, but carries it.

41. What Happened to Reason?

Reason has come in for a terrible beating in this century. The old skeptic denied that reason could know anything above the sensible world, the new skeptic denies he can know anything except what is below the sensible world, namely, in the unconscious. The characteristics of a decadent society, according to Palinurus in his "Unquiet Grave," are "luxury, skepticism, weariness and superstition." The author says that he himself is decadent, and because he is decadent, he is "skeptical." Franz Werfel tells how one image can alternate between old and new skepticism: "He finds only the external world in his inner world, i. e., a world without meaning and value. Consequently he turns away from his inner world because its emptiness is more painful than the emptiness of the factual world, which is at least relieved by noise and hubbub. As a harried exile of his own ego, he plunges into a sea of activity, whereby he creates false wants in the social life and causes a great deal of harm."

It used to be that men made a distinction between their judgments and their wishes. A man might wish his neighbor's wife, but he would make a judgment that he may not ever have her because it would be unjust. Judgments were grounded on evidence; wishes are grounded often only in emotions and passions. The new skeptics have denied that reason has any validity of its own; to their mind, reason does not lead to the discovery of truth — because there is no truth; its function to them is to provide "reasons" for thinking that the wishes should be satisfied. In the example given, the husband who covets his neighbor's wife will justify it on the ground that "he must live his own life" or that his "erotic contentment demands that she leave her husband." Reason thus becomes for the sex group of psychoanalysts always a rationalization for wishes, or a justification for our libido.

A person who rightly uses his reason, does so in order to take an impartial stock of the evidence, and insofar as it is possible, keeps his wishes, and, above all, his unconscious mind out of the whole business. But a sex-theorist who denies the capacity of reason to discover true purposes and goals makes reason the product of unconscious desires. A wife reasons when she tells her husband not to drop his ashes and throw his cigarette butts on the carpet; a husband rationalizes when he says that they are good for the carpet.

The overemphasis on the subconscious by the same psychoanalysts has done much to sap reason and kill intellectual curiosity. To say that character is to be found in the cellars of our existence and in the scrap heaps and garbage piles of the unconscious is to make the same mistake as believing that one can save a sinking ship by analyzing the water that pours into the hold. Such theorists must first use reason to destroy reason. If the theory is true that our characters are formed by our subconscious desires and libidos, then how can the theory ever be proven to be true? For anything to be true, there must be a correspondence between a belief about a certain thing and a fact, e g., Paris is in France.

But this peculiar theory of psychoanalysis, which holds that wishes and libidos constitute personality, has no objective reference at all. There is no France to which the belief about Paris may be referred. How are we to know that the psychoanalysts' interpretations of the dreams of a patient are true, since there is no external evidence by which they can be tested? The interpretations of the psychoanalysts are so arbitrary and subjective that each one gives different interpretations, except in the vague general agreement that "it has something to do with sex." If the psychoanalytic theory about reason is justified — namely that reason is only a rationalizing of our libido and sex desires — then there is no reason to take the theory seriously.

This idea that reason is the rationalization of our wishes is authoritarianism in its wildest form; it is the acceptance of an interpretation of a dream that cannot be tested in the objective world of facts. As Pascal wrote long ago, but for our time: "The most intolerable punishment for the human soul is to live with itself and think of itself alone." For that reason the soul is constantly concerned with the effort to forget itself, by occupying itself with all manner of things that prevent introspection. And this is the cause of all tumultuous activity.

42. How We Judge Anything

It is quite easy to calculate what will be the judgment of different groups of people on any moral issue which attracts public attention such as betraying the Government, using a military or political post for self-aggrandizement, or stealing another man's wife. One can predict the reaction on any moral problem with amazing exactness. Little do people realize how much they reveal their own character by the judgment they make on these moral issues.

The principle by which one predicts is the old Latin one which rendered literally is "whatever is received is received according to the manner of the one receiving it." If water is poured into a ditch, a glass, and a bonfire, the reaction will be quite different. So too if a truth is poured into a mind that is sincere, a mind that is indifferent, and a mind that is evil, the reception will be quite different. Why is it that children who receive exactly the same education vary so much? It is because they have a disposition or pattern made up of their choices, decisions, and desires which makes them act as differently as stomachs receiving the same food.

Actually it is not so much the knowledge that people have which determines their reaction, but their behavior; not the way they think, but the way they live. That is what Our Lord meant when He said: "Everyone who does evil hates the light, and doesn't come into the light lest his works be made known. But whoever does the truth comes to the light so his works may be revealed as wrought in God" (Jn 3:20-21). Here is the reason for every assault against morality and truth. "The flesh's way of thinking is hostile to God" (Rm 8:7). Is it wrong for students to cheat, to break a sworn code? Your answer depends on whether you do evil or whether you do good. In the text, Christ charges the want of faith to immorality. Men prefer darkness; therefore they hate the light.

No one hates the Gospel so long as he keeps it; but when it rebukes his evil deeds, then he hates it. Those who murder do not believe in the Fifth Commandment. The wicked can endure the Word so long as it does not gall their conscience and dig into their hearts. The drunkard does not cavil at a condemnation of hypocrisy, nor a profligate at a condemnation against avarice. The evil are in constant fear lest their actions be discovered to themselves, because that creates anxiety, guilt, and trouble. The truth robs men of the good opinion they had of themselves, so they are offended by it. A sluttish housemaid, when scolded at the untidiness of the rooms, said: "I am sure the rooms would be clean enough were it not for the sun which is always showing the dirty places." The good man on his way home at night wants the street well lighted; the robber hates the light because it reveals his evil presence. Religion is loved or hated for the same reason. It all depends on what we are bent on, goodness or evil. There is a blindness which is a result of evil passion, which, if continued, can make us odious of all truth. Agnosticism is not an intellectual position, but a moral position, or better still, an intellectual defense for a life which is afraid of the light.

He, however, who lives the truth has new horizons of truth constantly opening up before him. There are many who like to boast that they are looking for the truth, but they'd drop dead if they ever found it. They like to knock at its door, but they do not want the door opened, because truth creates responsibilities. Truth is not only objective, but subjective. It is objective because it is independent of us. Two plus two makes four whether we like it or not. It is subjective when we are so possessed by it that we do not cheat our neighbor by adding two and two to make three. As doctrine is the intellectual phase of Divine Truth, so obedience to it is its practical phase. Truth is not just something to be believed in, but to be acted out. Once we possess it, and it possesses us, we become something very different than we were before. The true life therefore is one which responds faithfully to all God's influences and which says in its joy: "My soul waits on the Lord" (Ps 33:20).

43. Right Attitude Toward Those Who Differ With Us

Everyone believes in the absoluteness of the multiplication table, and agrees that two and two makes four. Ibsen, however, once said: "Maybe two and two make five in the fixed stars." To this G.K. Chesterton retorted: "How do you know there are any such things as fixed stars, unless you keep adding over and over again, two and two make four?" Many persons adhere to certain causes with the same energy as they believe in the multiplication table, e.g., labor leaders, chambers of commerce, staunch Democrats, strong Republicans, etc. The greatest convictions are in the field of religion, though these actually in modern society provoke less social disturbance than economic conflicts among economic groups.

Why is it, on the one hand, when people

firmly believe some religious truth, that they often consider others who refuse to accept that same truth as either stupid or bigoted? Why is it too, on the other hand, that others who have no compass or map in life, and who deny there is any truth or goodness, other than that which they decide for themselves, take a position of cynicism and ridicule in face of the believer?

Here we are concerned not with deciding which group is right but what attitude one ought to take toward, first, his own convictions, and, second, to the convictions of others. The best answer to the first problem was offered over 1,500 years ago by St. Augustine: *"Sic ergo quaeramus tanquam inventuri, et sic inveniamus tanquam quaesituri."* "Seek the truth as one about to find it, and find it with the intention of always seeking it." Those who already have a philosophy are not to rest in idle adherence, but to keep on studying to deepen the knowledge one has, or else to discover that what he thought were profound truths were mere emotional adhesions or inherited prejudices without foundation either in history or in reason.

The second problem is the attitude to take toward those who differ with us. The answer is charity, love, benevolence and a recognition of the sincerity of motives and honesty of purposes of others. Sometimes this is called tolerance, but tolerance can be bad as well as good.

Tolerance is not right when its basic principle is a denial of truth and goodness and when it asserts that it makes no difference whether murder is a blessing or a crime, or whether a child should be taught to steal or to respect the rights of others.

But there can be another form of tolerance which is right, such as one inspired by true charity or love of God. Even though the virtuous may hold absolutely to their philosophy of life, they do so, not because they look down on the views of others as not as good as their own, but because their own beliefs are so real to them that they would not have anyone else hold them with less reason, less love and less devotion.

They then become like a mother who is very "intolerant" about the love of her child. It is not because she believes her child is prettier than any other child or more wise, but because she would have no other mother love her child less than she loves her. She would not want that mother to believe that her child was no different from a wolf, or that it was purely a matter of opinion whether the child should have love or not. Rather her love is so deep for her child, she wants others to love just as much, and in that bond of love they will be one.

There is too often a tendency to condemn any opinion of a group or a race or class, simply because it belongs to them. A spirit of charity would suggest a willingness to search for the truth in their position, or at least to give it as kindly an interpretation as possible. There is something good in everything. Evil has no capital of its own; it lives in goodness as a parasite. But loving the partial goodness in others we bring them more quickly to the circle of Goodness which is God. This was the tactic of Our Lord when He spoke to an adulteress at the well. There was nothing in common between His Divine Goodness and her sinful life, except a love of a drink of cold water So He started there... and led her on to a declaration that He was Love and Savior of the world.

44. How "Open" Minds Close

Nothing is more interesting in our social scene than to see how often those who boast of an "open mind" end with a closed one. People with an infernal pride will sometimes take the lowest places in order to attract attention; so often those who boast that their minds are in a state of suspension until they find truth are often those who are most impervious to it. The open mind is commendable when it is open like a road that leads to a city which is its destination. But the open mind is condemnable when it is like an abyss or a manhole. Those who boast of their open-mindedness are invariably those who love to search for truth but not to find it; they love the chase but not the capture; they admire the footprints of truth, but not catching up with it. They go through life talking about "widening the horizons of truth" but without ever seeing the sun.

The discovery of truth can be very embarrassing. For example, to awaken at night to discover that we are really very selfish and egotistic. Truth brings with it great responsibilities; that is why so many keep their hands open to welcome it, but never close them to grasp it. The real thinker who is willing to embrace a truth at all costs generally has double price to pay — first, isolation from current opinion or the mass mind. Any one who arrives at the moral conclusion that divorce prepares the way for the breakdown of civilization must be prepared to be ostracized by the Herods and the Salomes of this world. Non-conformity with the mass mind can be expected to bring down upon the offender's head opposition and ridicule. Second, those who discover a truth must stand naked before the uplifted stroke of its duties or else take up the cross that it imposes. These two effects of embracing truth, one negative which is opposition, the other positive, which is the burden of the new idea, make many people fearful. In their cowardice, they keep their minds "open" so they will never have to close on anything that would entail responsibility, duty, moral correction or altered behavior.

This is the reason. The "open" mind does not want truth because truth implies duty. A farmer's son will avoid passing the woodpile because he knows if he passes it, he ought to bring in some firewood to his mother. That truth creates a duty which he wishes to avoid. Responsibility is the one thing the "open mind" is most anxious to avoid. Avoiding truth is only negative; people cannot long endure in that attitude. So they seek about for something which will completely relieve them from responsibility. The avoidance of responsibility, though, only results in tyranny, the abdication of one's free will to another, whether it be to an ideology or a dictator. The only real solution is for those with "open minds" to close on truth, even though it does involve a change in behavior, for ultimately it is truth, and only truth, which can make them free.

45. Silence

We live in the most talkative age in the history of the world. It would take ten or fifteen million men in previous ages to communicate to others the same information which one person today provides in a single broadcast. The love of noise and excitement in modern civilization is due in part to the fact that people are unhappy on the inside. Noise exteriorizes them, distracts them, and makes them forget their worries at least for the moment. There is an unmistakable connection between an empty life and a hectic pace. To make progress the world must have action, but it must also know *why* it is acting and that requires thought, contemplation, and silence.

The world is in danger of becoming like a turnstile that is in everybody's way but stops nobody; it is a place where we look into everything but see nothing. Felix Frankfurter tells the effect of excessive talkativeness on government; everything is done under blare and noise, the deliberative process is impaired and government becomes too susceptible to quick thinking. It is, I believe, of deep significance that the Constitution of the United States was written behind closed doors, and it is well to remember that earth was thrown on the streets of Philadelphia to protect the Convention from the noise of traffic. It might also he added that when the Apostles received the Holy Spirit it was behind closed doors too, and after they kept nine days of silence awaiting the coming of heavenly Wisdom.

Action is the great need of the Eastern World; silence, the need of the Western. The East with its fatalism does not believe that man does anything; the West with its actionism believes that man does everything. Somewhere in between is the golden mean wherein silence prepares for action. He who holds his tongue for a day will speak much more wisely tomorrow. Even friendships are matured in silence. Friends are made by words; love is preserved in silence. The best friends are those who know how to keep the same silences. As Maeterlinck wrote: "Speech is too often not, as the Frenchman defined it, the art of concealing Thought, but a quiet stifling and suspending Thought, so that there is none to conceal... Speech is of time; Silence of Eternity."

The Ancient Spartans used to say that "a fool cannot be silent" and the Scriptures say that "a fool's voice is known by many words" (Ec 5:3). It is all very well to plaster our church lawn with placards saying: "Leave the world better than you find it," but we will never leave the world better until through silence, contemplation and prayer we improve ourselves. We must leave the world to help the world. That life is most effectively lived which every now and then withdraws from the scene of action to contemplation where one learns the terrible defeat and futility which come from excessive absorption in detail and action.

Throughout the United States there is growing what is known as the "Retreat Movement" in which busy men and women betake themselves over a weekend to a quiet place in the country where they spend time in silence, prayer and purging their consciences. The ancient Romans used to keep a bowl outside the business house, and whenever they left it at the close of day they washed their hands as if to imply they even washed their hands of their business.

In silence, there is humility of spirit or what might be called a "wise passivity." In such the ear is more important than the tongue. God speaks, but not in cyclones — only in the zephyrs and gentle breezes. As the scientist learns by sitting passively before nature, so the soul learns wisdom by being responsive to His Will. The scientist does not tell nature its laws; nature tells the scientist. We do not tell or impose our will on God; in silence like Mary, we await an Annunciation.

From this, learn the lesson that those who would become wise must become silent. A mirror is silent, yet it reflects forests, sunsets, flowers and faces. Great ascetic souls, given to years of meditation, have taken on a radiance and a beauty which are beyond the outlines of face. They seem to reflect, like the mirror on the outside, the Christ they bear within. What is really important is what happens within us, not outside us. The rapidity of communication, the hourly news broadcasts, tomorrow's news the night before — all these make people live on the surface of their souls. The result is that very few live inside themselves. They have their moods determined by the world. Instead of carrying their own atmosphere with them, as the earth does as it revolves around the sun, they are like barometers that register every change in the world outside. Silence alone can give them an inner sanctuary into which they may retire for repose, as hidden gardens wherein like Adam and Eve before the Fall they walk with God in the cool of evening.

Only in solitariness is true spirituality born, when the soul stands naked before its God. In that moment these are the only two realities in the universe. In this discovery is born love of neighbor, for then we love our fellow human beings, not because of what they can do for us, but because we see that they too are real or potential children of God. Though truth is not personal, we make it personal by contemplation.

YOU

46. Pleasures

Pleasure is very peculiar: to possess it one must not seek it directly, but rather seek it through something else. Not even an avid cocktail drinker takes a cocktail to have pleasure; rather, he has pleasure because he takes a cocktail. Pleasure does not cause itself, but is caused by the possession of some good or the attainment of some purpose.

Our complex modern society is directed to the creation of mass entertainment rather than individual pleasure. Movies, television, advertising are geared to the masses, and generally to their lowest common denominator. Their aim is to satisfy what all have in common, rather than what they have individually. It is much easier to find a television program on a prize fight than one on Shakespeare. As the English philosopher, C.E.M. Joad put it, "Those things which are peculiar to each of us and may in their forms of expression well be different in all of us cannot be catered for in bulk by commercial agencies." When you want to enjoy an individual pleasure, even though it be but an hour of chamber music in the privacy of your own room, or a page of Pepys' *Diary*, you must isolate yourself from those who cater to the mob.

Most pleasures today are associated with movement and in the case of the young, with speed.

A quick change of scenery and pace seems to be one of the ingredients of modern enjoyment. One out of every four persons in the United States changes his address during the year. The unquiet mind makes an unquiet body. Novelists move more than philosophers or thinkers, because the novelists generally write about sense-experiences while philosophers write about thoughts. Socrates never left Greece, Kant was never outside Koenigsberg, Bach was permanently at Leipzig while Schubert spent most of his life around Vienna. But today many novelists leave their country in search of new experiences. There is some connection between stationariness of the body and the acquisition of the superior truths of the spirit. It is only the quiet pool that reflects the stars.

After a body is surfeited with pleasures, it reaches a point where there is less satisfaction in the pleasure than in the pursuit of it. Not to be someplace, but the thrill of speeding there, becomes the goal of life. Joyce Kilmer in his delightful poem "Pennies" pictures a boy holding some pennies in his hand. The pleasure of getting them is all gone and he is bored with their possession. Suddenly he drops his pennies; seeing them scatter and roll about, all his zest for acquiring returns. When the pennies no longer satisfied, he substituted the new pleasure of hunting them. There is not a millionaire who did not say: "I will retire when I get a million." The million bored him; only then did he realize that his pleasure was not in having money, but in pursuing it.

As the human mind loses an objective and a goal in life, even its culture becomes identified with movement as pleasure, instead of the attainment of a goal. Modern writing reflects this inasmuch as it is made up of experiences strung together, but leading nowhere, nor painting any moral. Minds never inquire where they came from, or where they are going; they are just on the way. They never begin, they never develop, they never end — they just stop. Nothing in life has a shape, a pattern, a rule or destiny. Nothing links things together except more succession in time; the needle of writing is drawn through the cloth but it weaves no pattern.

One cannot talk with the mouth full. Our thinking processes are impeded in direct relation to the intensity of the exercise of our sensible satisfactions. The more intense the sensible reaction, the less the concentration of thought. This is the basis for two important truths: first, lust does, as Scripture says, impede the spirit and the mind. The second is that the pleasures of the body do play an important role in aiding the soul. It is this very power of relaxation attached to sensible pleasure which proves such a boon; it rests our soul, and when pleasure does that, it is really pleasurable.

47. The Psychology of Man and Woman

Education today makes no difference between the training of man and woman. This is right from the point of view of opportunities that are open to both, but it is shortsighted when one considers the psychological differences between the two.

The first obvious difference between the two, and the one most often pointed out, is that man is rational and woman intuitive. A man often stands bewildered and confused at what are called a "woman's reasons." They completely escape his understanding, because they cannot be analyzed, taken apart and arranged in an orderly sequence. Her conclusions seem to come as a "whole piece"; there are no vestibules to the house of her arguments; you walk right into the parlor of a conclusion and, it seems, often by a trap door. The very immediacy of her conclusions startles a man because they obtrude without any apparent foundation. But they are just as unshakable as the reasoned deduction of the male.

A second difference is that a man governs the home, but the woman reigns in it. Government is related to justice and law; reigning, to love and feeling. The orders of the father in a home are like written mandates from a king; the influence of the woman, however, is more subtle, more felt and less aggressive. The commands of the father are more jerky and intermittent; the quiet pervading radiation of the mother is constant, like the growth of a plant. And yet both are essential for the home, for justice without love could become tyranny, and love without justice could become toleration of evil.

A third difference is how they react as on one hand to trifles, such as the souring of cream and, on the other hand the great crises such as the loss of a job. Man is much less disturbed by trifles, with the exception of the morning paper being taken by the neighbor's dog. The daily shocks of life disturb man less, the little things are like drops of water he can absorb in the sponge of his masculinity. The woman, however, is more readily upset by inconsequential things, possessed as she is by a rare talent of turning molehills into mountains.

But when it comes to the great crises of life, it is the woman, in virtue of her gentle power of reigning who can give great consolation to man in his troubles. She can recover reason and good sense at the very moment the man seems to lose his. When the husband is remorseful, sad, and disquieted, she brings comfort and assurance. As the ocean is ruffled on the surface but calm in the depths, so in a home, the man is the rippled surface, the woman the deep and quiet stability.

A fourth difference is that woman is less satisfied with mediocrity than man. This may be because man is more attached to the material and the mechanical, and woman more to the biological and the living. The closer one gets to the material, the more one becomes materialized. Nothing so dulls the soul for the inner values of life as counting. But the woman, being the bearer of life, is less indifferent to great values, more quickly disillusioned with the material and the human. This may account for the judgment often made that religion is more natural for women than for men. This is not because woman is more timid and is more likely to seek flight and refuge in the spiritual, it is rather because being less trapped by the material, she is more likely to pursue ideals that transcend the earthly.

These differences, instead of being opposites, are actually in a marriage correlated. Man is like the roots of a plant; woman more like the blossom that bears the fruit. One is in communion with the earth and business; the other with the sky and life. One is related to time, the other to eternity. The fusion of both is the prolongation into the home of the Incarnation where Eternity became time and the Word became flesh, and the Divine became the human in the person of Christ. Differences are not irreconcilable; rather, they are complimentary qualities. The functional differences correspond with certain psychic differences, which make one in relation to the others like the violin and the bow, producing the music of a home and the joys of a marriage that symbolize the mystical marriage of Christ and His Bride, the Church.

48. The Dark Side of Good

Because of cold wars, high taxes, threats of inflation, and general insecurity, we have become accustomed to take a dark view of the world. There is some justification for this, for never before in the history of Christian civilization was there ever such a mass attack on decency, honor, personal rights and freedom as there is at the present hour. While there is justification for looking on the dark side because of evil, there is, however, no justification for the present tendency to look upon the dark side of good. It is one thing to be gloomy about starvation, but it is quite another matter to be gloomy about good health; disease has its shadows, but why see shadows in health? In a word, why is it that so many see the dark side of virtue, goodness, honesty, purity and honor?

In other ages, though men lost virtue, they still admired it; though they ran from the battlefield at the first need of courage, they still admired the hero who fought and suffered; though they threw away the map of the roadway of life, they never denied the need of a map. But, in our generation, men look for shadow in the radiance of every virtue. Love of truth is called harshness and intolerance; purity is called abnormality or fear of totems or myths; humility is termed weakness; the meek are made to appear as lacking in force and strength; those who pray and believe in God are labeled "escapists"; the generous are accused of seeking acclaim; the contemplative are sneered at as "useless," the husband of one wife and a devoted father of a family is "in a rut."

A civilization can he forgiven for seeing the dark side of evil, but should it not examine its conscience when it begins to fear the dark side of the good? The right and normal reaction when one sees a shadow is to think of the light; in fact, the darker the shadow the brighter the light. Goodness needs but little explanation, for good is self-propagating and self-explanatory; it is the evil, darkness, and suffering which need explanation. One does not only conclude to the existence of God because there are good things in the world; but one argues that because there is evil in the world, therefore there must be a God, for evil is a parasite on goodness. It has no capital of its own. Darkness is not a positive entity; darkness is the absence of light and is intelligible only in terms of light. Most of the suffering of the world is intelligible in terms of the abuse of something that is so profoundly good that not even

God will take it away for all eternity, and that is our freedom.

Whence then comes the tendency to see the bad in things, if it be not that our consciences are already so burdened with guilt and hidden distortions that to ease them we have to minimize the good in others and drag them down to the level of the worst or else reduce heroism to mediocrity. Public officials are thought to be best described, when not the good that they do is recounted, but when some suspicion or slur is cast upon their characters. The kettles are unhappy unless they call the pots black.

How our outlook on the world would change if the makers of public opinion, instead of seeing the dark side of the evil alone, would see the bright side of the good; if they would single out politicians, business men, labor leaders, parents and others who mirror forth great virtues and moral integrity, then the evil of the world would be more quickly overcome. When pestilence is abroad, it is encouraging to know that there are recoveries and there are many who are not stricken. But if our doctors are accused of being diseased and our teachers are accused of ignorance; if our public officials are all crooks, then who shall hope?

We do not make children give up writing because they spill the ink. The world is discouraged enough; it needs encouragement, inspiration, good example; above all, it will be happier when it sees a standard and a Redeemer Who invites us away from the dark side: "I am the Light of the world; whoever follows Me shall not walk in darkness" (Jn 8:12).

49. Where Character Is Made

Hardly anyone today challenges the view that character is made by outside or external influences, such as home background, schooling, poverty or wealth, the propaganda to which an individual was subjected and the neighborhood in which he was raised. This view could lead to the destruction of responsibility if carried to extremes — and responsibility, it must not he forgotten, is the mark of freedom. Environmental influences only condition, but they do not cause character. Our Lord put His finger on the cause when He said: "From the heart come wicked thoughts, murder, adultery, fornication, theft, false witness, and blasphemy. These things are what make a person unclean" (Mt 15:19).

Modern psychology emphasizes the importance of the subconscious, but the Divine Master stresses rather the conscious factor of the intellect and will, that is, our knowledge and our decisions.

The combination of these two is sometimes called the heart, and from them comes our character, as from the tree comes its fruits.

The heart is the mint wherein the coinage of human life is stamped; it is the anvil which forges habits and routines; it is the "stick" which pilots the plane of life. Sir Walter Scott once said to his son-in-law Lockhart: "We shall never learn to feel and respect our own calling and destiny, until we have taught ourselves to consider everything as moonshine, compared with the education of the heart."

The reform of outward conduct and environment is essential, and it is to this that much civil law is ordained. But it really only deals with the effects and not with the causes; social reformation is only superficial, it is like cutting off the tops of the weeds while the roots are left in the ground. Much social reform attempts to cure problems such as crime and juvenile delinquency by changing environment, such as building more dance halls and swimming pools. One of the difficulties social reform must always face is that it hardly ever goes into operation until things have gotten very bad. As long as the people are not aroused to abuses or evil, they will not support social legislation. It must be remembered that all crimes against society are founded on false and wicked ideas, and until these are altered, society will not be altered. A lion is not gentle once it is behind a cage; a wild horse is not less ill-tempered because of a bridle and kicking stirrups put on it.

Only in a limited sense is it true that circumstances make us who we are; they do so only to the extent that we permit them to form us. It is not so much the outward that influences the inward, as the inward that influences the outward. If the reservoir is to be kept clean, all the streams that pour into it must be pure. Evil has its roots in the heart. "As a man thinks in his heart, so he is" (Pr 23:7). The stalactite pillars to be found in caves give a perfect example of how habits are formed by thoughts. Water on the surface of the earth sinks through the soil and the rocks, carrying with it a tiny sediment. These drops fall from the ceiling of the cave to the floor, but as they fall they form an icicle, and little by little the deposit grows into a stone pillar. In like manner, if the thoughts and desires and wishes of the heart carry with them a deposit of our decisions and our thoughts, and if these are evil it will not be long until they build strong pillars of evil habits on the outside; the opposite is true when the thoughts are good thoughts and are holy and pure.

It is the things that we like that make our character; life is stained only because the heart is impure. Thoughts are the eggs of words, and when the will gives motive power to evil thoughts, they become actual transgressions. No man would be believed who, holding a bucket of muddy water in his hand, said that he drew it from a spring that was crystal clear. The heart is the center of life, the throne where manhood sits and rules; the subconscious holds the thoughts and the desires that have been discarded or else the reflections and desires of the heart that have passed into action. Evil is not a robber that breaks into our house; it is a tenant to whom the house has been rented. But, on the contrary, if we keep our hearts clean and God-like on the inside, we will change our environment.

50. Memory

Memory is one of the most neglected factors in modern education. In previous generations children had to memorize poetry, irregular verbs, and important historical dates, and such is still the case in many European schools. Perhaps the neglect of memory is in part due to the modern contempt of anything that implies effort, discipline and application. But the penalties are terrific as businessmen go madly searching for typists who can spell.

God has blessed some people with remarkable powers of retention. It is said that Themistocles knew by heart the names of twenty thousand citizens of Athens. History records that Cyrus knew the name of every soldier in his army. On the other hand, Aristotle held that people who have such vivid memories for details never have good judgment. This may be because images pile up with such rapidity as to destroy the relation between abstract ideas which are essential for judgment.

Lord Bacon and Coleridge both held that nothing that is impressed on the memory ever leaves it. This is evident in persons who in old age are brought before the scenes of their childhood, and immediately names, places and incidents come out from their storehouse of memory and the past is lived again. As old palimpsests bear the original writing under dust or new messages, so the memory retains all that we have seen and heard, said and done. Today is but the product of all our yesterdays, and our present is but the harvest of the past. The fragments of our memory are very much like islands for the moment unconnected. But it may be that they are continuous, as the solid earth itself is continuous if one did but drain off the water from the seas.

Hidden in this retentive power of memory may also be the basis of what will be our final judgment, for what is memory but an infallible autobiography? As at the end of the day the businessman takes out of the cash register a record of all the debits and the credits, so at the end of life the memory offers the basis of how we shall be judged. As Coleridge put it: "And this perchance is the dread

book of judgment, in whose mysterious hieroglyph-
ics every idle word is recorded. Yes, in the very nature of a living spirit, it may be more possible that
heaven and earth should pass away than that a single
act, a single thought, should be loosened from that
living chain of causes, to all those links, conscious
or unconscious, the free will, our own absolute self,
is coextensive and co-present."

Memory is the source of unhappiness to many
people today; hence their attempts to stifle it with
alcohol and drugs. What is the explanation for the
vast amount of sleeping tablets sold to the American public? It has been pointed out that enough are
sold to put every person in the United States to sleep
twenty-two nights a year, or to put nine million
people to sleep three hundred and sixty-five nights
a year. Undoubtedly, some of this is medically necessary for the easing of pain, but more likely most
of the pills are taken in an effort to "forget" or "get
away from it all." The memory has the peculiar trick
of never asking our permission for anything it shoots
up into consciousness; sometimes the more displeasing the ideas are, and the harder we try to forget them, the quicker and the more often they flash
before our eyes. It is a psychological fact that the
more the mind fears a thing, the more that fearful
thing comes like a ghost out of the past to torture
it. What we hate and dread we remember best, and
nothing that we present to our mind can blot it out.

No wonder Macbeth in desperation asked his physician: "Canst thou not… pluck from the memory a rooted sorrow; raze out the written troubles of the brain… which weigh upon the heart?" (*Macbeth*, Act V, Scene iii, Line 40).

What is driving people to sleeping tablets is to some extent driving them to psychoanalytical couches — they are in flight from what is distasteful and what cannot be blotted out — and most often it is unrequited guilt. We point out these sad facts to remind those who are full of fears and anxieties that there is another remedy besides sleeping tablets, and that is consciously confronting our guilt and asking the pardon of God. Another way is to live right, so we won't have to try to forget.

51. How Things Go Wrong

It is easy to understand why an alcoholic gets drunk, a robber steals again, and an unhappy man criticizes others. But why is it that an habitually sober man may get drunk, a kind person be cruel to another, and an otherwise devoted husband be unfaithful to his wife?

To answer these questions one must make a study of the ideals and the objects which move the will to action. There are two kinds of stimuli or excitants to action — one is called adequate, the other inadequate. In the sensible order, the adequate stimulus of sight is color; the inadequate stimulus may be a red barn; the adequate stimulus of hearing is sound; the inadequate may be a policeman's whistle; the adequate stimulus of curiosity is a strange object which excites wonder; an inadequate object may be a mink coat over baggy slacks. Such improper objects delight or arouse us for the moment, but do not bring complete satisfaction or happiness.

Every faculty or talent we have has some object which is its complete realization, for example, the perfection or adequate object of the mind is truth; the perfection or adequate object of the will is goodness. One single truth such as the knowledge of the electrical charges inside an atom, does not completely satisfy the mind, because the mind is made to know the full orbit of truth, not a segment of it. A good meal satisfies the stomach, but a good deed does not exhaust the possibilities of the will; it remains incomplete until the highest and best of its ideals are fulfilled.

If the human mind were suddenly presented with the fullness of truth, that is to say, with Divine Truth which contains within itself all that is knowable and can be known, it would not be free to reject it, because it is for that that the mind was made and which alone can satisfy it. It is like a man finding the ideal woman whom he wants to be his wife. No other can satisfy once the ideal has been discovered. If the will were brought face to face with Divine Love, and saw it dying in a human nature for others, it would be irresistibly drawn to it. In heaven, there will be no more freedom of choice, because once in possession of the perfect, there will be nothing left to desire. And yet, one will still be perfectly free because he has become one with Love and Power that can do all things.

On this earth, we are not confronted with this total object of our existence, which is God; we are pulled hither and thither by imperfect objects, false ideals, and tin gods. Nothing that we see or hear or know is so compelling as to be a magnet pulling us irresistibly toward that which is the perfection of our personality.

Now we are in a position to answer the question posed above. We, being free in our choices, may often substitute an inadequate for an adequate idea; we may deliberately drive off the road though we have the road map before us; we may hit a sour note though the score of music is in front of our eyes. Hot objects are normally required to stimulate heat spots on the skin, but these may sometimes be stimulated by a cold bar of iron on a cold day so that we get the impression of "heat." As skin sometimes mistakes cold for hot, particularly when the eyes are closed, so too a person who blacks out his reason and faith for the moment may substitute a false good for a true good. The drug addict and the alcoholic on the contrary, have deliberately determined to pursue a "good" which does not lead to perfect happiness; their means are always wrong. It is like deliberately choosing half a baby to the whole baby. The only way they can be deterred is by placing before them adequate goals which satisfy the whole personality and not a part of it. In the case of the otherwise sober man who gets drunk, there is here only momentary substitution of a false ideal. Generally, the unhappiness that he feels is enough to bring him back again to his senses and the pursuit of the highest ideals. If people only knew it, the emptiness and the void they feel after subscribing to false ideals is really the voice of God saying: "You are on the wrong road. Come back! I am the Way, the Truth and the Life."

FAITH

52. *For Those Who Work for God*

Those who are working for the acquiring of a fortune, or to enjoy life, or maybe to exist, will approach work from an entirely different point of view than the one who works for God. The peculiar characteristic of the latter is that when he has rendered it all he may not indulge in any self-complacency as if he had done anything extraordinary or deserved any special commendation, for everything that is done belongs to God. There will be no whimpering over his lot or complaining that it is tremendously hard as if he were undergoing a species of martyrdom. On the other hand, he will not be looking for any extraordinary reward as if it were that which was sought rather than the service of the One we love.

The difference between those who labor for themselves and those who labor for God is the difference between a hired servant in the house and a son or a daughter who works out of love for his or her parents. When the life of a mother is hanging in the balance no one can persuade a daughter or a son to take rest. All standards of duty and "enoughness" and legalism are destroyed and transcended by love. A love transforms work to such an extent that it almost ceases to be work where there is love. So long as our work is merely the carrying out of another's orders it will tend to become mechanical and methodical. But the moment we become identified in spirit with our work, the moment the work becomes the expression of the great idea and the instrument of sympathy and affection, above all, when it takes on the character of a passion or an enthusiasm, it overlaps all mechanical bounds.

Sick patients always feel very differently toward the physician when he visits and charges for it, than when he visits saying: "I just dropped in to see how you were." Our Blessed Lord had no word of thanks for the grumbling slave who grudges the service at table after the day's ploughing. Those who love the master never even think of sacrifice. Nothing can be called a sacrifice which is simply paid back as a small part of a debt which is owed to God and which never can be repaid. The very moment we grow complacent about our work, our work spoils in our hands. We begin to think of ourselves instead of our work, of the wonders that we have achieved instead of the toils that lie before us and how best we can discharge them. As soon as complaint about our lot and our task begins, as soon as we protest that our burdens are too heavy, we immediately unfit ourselves for them, make them more formidable than before and ourselves less competent to do them.

Honesty of intention, purity and sincerity of motives, the cheerfulness with which we address ourselves to our work, all count more before God than the amount of work that we do. He said that we should be content even to wait at the Master's table after we had ploughed the soil and fed the cattle. Though the time of our eating and drinking may come later, we shall work then for His Glory, thus eating our bread with gladness and singleness of heart, not for enjoyment alone but that we may gain new strength for serving Him. Creation alone, not to speak of Redemption, places us under a debt to God which our most accurate creditors can never discharge. If our best services cannot discount His past favors, much less can we plead them for the future. Whatever encouragement He gives as an annex to our obedience will be acknowledged as a pure bounty of grace and love.

There is a beautiful story told about the great Spartan Brasidas. When he complained that Sparta was a small state, his mother said to him: "Son, Sparta has fallen to your lot and it is your duty to adorn it." We are all workers of this world and regardless of the lot in which we are cast, the duty is ever the same — to adorn it.

53. Inner Nakedness

An eternally feminine problem is always: "What will I wear?" It probably began the day after the initial rebellion, when Eve looked up at the leaves of the fig tree and said: "I wonder which one I will wear today?" Or it may have been that she turned to Adam and said: "I haven't a stitch to my name." In any case, it is interesting to note that in the account of the Fall, given in the Book of Genesis, Adam and Eve were not conscious of the need of clothes until after they had sinned. Very likely there had been an effulgence of their soul shining through their bodies which became as garments of radiance. Perhaps the glory attendant upon Christ on the Mountain of the Transfiguration was His Divinity shining through His humanity. So, too, the inner holiness of our First Parents was in a certain sense their garment not made with hands. After that inner beauty of the soul was lost, there was need of outer clothing. Once naked on the inside, external covering was necessary. Clothed originally with grace and holiness, there was no sense of nakedness, either inside or out.

Modern psychology has recovered this truth hidden in the First Book of the Bible. Its expression of the truth is that excessive luxury on the outside is often a sign of nothing on the inside. "Defensive mechanisms" are attempts to hide some failing, defect, or spiritual nakedness. For example, a young woman who wants to appear learned will cultivate an accent, use the jargon of the intelligentsia, and begin conversations with: "Oh, you never read Professor Schlamz' book on 'The subaltern relationship of the Id to the Sex-Libido in the introverted schizophrenics'?" How often, too, the man who has made a lot of money, either through oil spouting in his face or through unearned increment in real estate, will try to cover up his ignorance or his intellectual nakedness by considering all talk except money as a "waste of time."

This love of display to hide moral and spiritual nudity thus manifests itself in negative fashion. College students, seeking to make up for a want of recognition, will seek to attract attention by wearing loud clothes. Bad clothes, baggy and misfitting garments will sometimes be worn to solicit the eyes of others. This is an old trick. Centuries ago, Plato, a man of taste who had fine carpets in his home, was visited by Diogenes, who lived in a tub and said disagreeable things about others because they were not as poor as he. One day, Diogenes in an ill temper came to visit Plato and stamping on the carpets said: "I trample on the pride of Plato." "Yes," said Plato, "and with greater pride."

The soul has its apparel as well as the body, and the psychologists are right in saying that exaggerated display on the outside is a sign of barrenness within. The external first meets the eye, and there is a natural tendency to judge the contents by the wrappings; diamonds wrapped in a newspaper clipping would be suspected of worthlessness. But this does not diminish the value of the inner man. "Keeping clean the outside of the cup while the inside was full of filth and corruption" provoked some of the sternest words of Our Divine Lord (cf. Mt 23:25). Those who keep up the externals only to cover up the internal are like some of the ancient Egyptian temples that were magnificent on the outside, but on the inside had only the image of a serpent or a crocodile.

There is much wisdom and peace hidden in the counsel of a third century writer who, talking to a group of young women, said, "Clothe yourselves with the silk of piety, with the satin of sanctity, and with the purple of modesty, and you will have God Himself as your suitor."

54. Cares

The world and modern man are learning the same lesson in the present crisis, namely, the helplessness of either to save self. A century and a half of pride has made modern man feel that the burden is on himself alone, and that if he steps from under it there must be a crash. This kind of pride begets the greatest despair, for in a crisis it can appeal to nothing outside itself.

It may well be that the world at the present time is being humbled that we may learn that trusting in God is something else besides an inscription on a penny. God, of course, does not hold out His arms to our burden without our cooperation. Casting all our care on God is casting self on God, for self is our worst care. As a parent will not for a time help his son with his studies, if he in the beginning said he could learn them by himself, so God sometimes shuts Himself up from us until we are sorely in need of help. Even then God does not force our will, but He wills that we should look squarely at the importance of self and acknowledge that we have used up all our capital, that the world cannot help us, and that we have nothing in heaven or on earth but God. The bitterest draught we will ever drink is the confession of our utter inadequacy. The world says that at this moment we are at our worst; actually we are at our best. We are at our worst if we fall into despair; but we are at our best if humbled we cry to God for help.

The words of Our Divine Lord: "He who humbles himself shall be exalted, and he who exalts himself shall be humbled" (Mt 23:12) express sound psychological insights as well as a spiritual fact. How often we see a man endowed with more conceit than ability, more self-confidence than resources conducting some important business. His very exaltation brings out his humiliation, his height accentuates his nothingness.

On the other hand, those who have swallowed their pride, confessed their inability to perform great tasks, from that moment on grow in the esteem of men. The sporting world traditionally loves the "underdog." In the boxing world the little fighter with the small odds wins the crowd by his courage. Comedians too "exalt" themselves by allowing their "straight man" or guest star to "humble" them. The lowly violet that grows close to the earth is more praised by poets than the sunflower that always turns its head to the spotlight.

The humble cast their cares upon God — such cares as business and family problems, frequent misunderstandings with their neighbors and the culture of their own soul. There would be much less anxiety in the world if people would see that trials are often permitted by an allowing Providence to purify us from sin, to detach us from what is harmful. Fellow creatures generally do not want our cares, for they have enough of their own. Only God is left to be solicitous of our cares. Throwing them upon Him is done in two ways: by prayers and by faith. Prayer tells God what care is; faith believes that God can and will lift it. No one can cast his cares upon an "it." If there is ever to be a relief for the burdens of the human heart, there must be behind the universe something more than a vague Power, namely, a loving Father. He who cares for the sparrows, the lilies of the field and knows even the fall of a strand of hair from the head, will not indeed be unmindful of us toward whom He made the greatest act of love this world has ever seen (Lk 12:22-34).

Some wrongly believe the proper thing to do with cares is to try to banish them from our mind and to seek pleasures in order to forget them. But it is not easy to ignore anxieties. Dr. Johnson's cure for toothache — to treat it with contempt — is all right for those who have no toothache. Then, too, pleasures indulged in too much beget their own cares. The greatest care of all, which is a feeling of personal guilt the denial of which has produced so many mental upsets, can be relieved only by throwing ourselves on an allowing God. Aristotle said men would laugh if they were told to cast their cares on Jupiter, for his work was only to shake the heavens as a thunderer, not to draw men to him in their woes.

To solve our cares God must not only be Personal, He must also be in the dust of human cares. That is why He with full understanding of our troubles can say: "Come to Me, all you who labor and are heavily burdened, and I will refresh you" (Mt 11:28).

55. Humility

Certain words pass out of our vocabulary until some incident or writer digs them up as forgotten treasures. One such word is "Humility." But often it happens that when words signifying great forgotten virtues are resurrected, they are used in an entirely new sense. For example, in China those who refuse to accept the domination of the government are accused of being wanting in "humility." The cat that rebels against being devoured by the mouse is also labelled as failing in that virtue.

Humility does not mean letting other people walk over you; humility is not passivity, submissiveness, nor under-estimation of oneself; it is not condemnation, nor a belittling of oneself; it is not an enemy of greatness striving for the stars, for when God became man He gave the counsel: "Be perfect as your Heavenly Father is perfect" (Mt 5:48). Humility is not a self-awareness that one is humble, for then it becomes pride; humility is not a self-contempt that prepares for gloom, or cynicism, nor is it believing that our talents are less valuable than they really are. A man six foot three who is praised for being so tall is not humble when he says: "Oh no, I am really only four feet four."

Humility is truth about ourselves; it is a virtue by which one does not esteem himself to be more than he really is. It therefore avoids an inordinate love of one's own excellence, and an inordinate pleasure in seeing others inferior to self. To see oneself as one really is, means that we must never mistake the imaginary self for the real self. The real self is what we are before God and before ourselves in an examination of conscience. Take an opera singer of undoubted excellence; she is not humble if she says: "Really, I can't sing a note." Rather her humility will consist in recognizing that she has received a tremendous endowment of a voice, and she will thank God for it. But the recognition of this truth must be counterbalanced by a recognition of her limitations. Because she thinks she is a good singer, she must not think she is necessarily a good acrobat. Humility holds her soul back lest she attempt the impossible. This is the great failing of those who have one talent. How often the scientist because he knows experimental facts, is asked about a belief in immortality or belief in God — and with no humility parades as a master of all subjects because he is master of one.

Humility has a positive and a negative side. The positive side is living up to one's capacities and abilities — carpenters being good carpenters, baseball players being good baseball players, comedians being funny comedians, and physicists being good physicists. But humility in its negative side will keep them from overshooting their mark and morticians will not be comedians at funerals, theologians will not be scientists, and scientists will not be theologians. Humility, then, moderates our appetite for perfection, but it does not destroy it.

No one is humble who does not believe in God, and who does not recognize dependence on the Power that created him, the Love that redeemed him and the Spirit that sanctified him. Our imperfection in the face of God has its immediate compensation in the fact that God Who made us creatures will, with our cooperation, make us His children. Once humbled we become exalted, living no longer on the human level, but enjoying the glorious liberty of the children of God. In relation to neighbor, we look for the best that is in him, and for the worst that is in ourselves. This enables us to purge ourselves of our faults and to imitate the good qualities of our neighbor.

Children in a family without love become rebellious, recalcitrant, stubborn, selfish and cruel. Adults who live in a loveless or Godless world end in despair which is the last extreme of self-love. Those who are loved become kind, ready for service and quick to love others. The humble will then never be overcome by praise; they accept praise to return it to God. *Fecit mihi magna, qui potens est, et sanctum nomen ejus.* "He Who is mighty has done great things for me, and holy is *His* name" (Lk 1:49).

56. Moods

At one time, it was believed that the sun moved about the earth; indeed, it did seem so to the eye, as we saw it purpling the dawn, and at night "setting like a host in the flaming monstrance of the West." But now we know that the earth moves about the sun.

As there were two ways of looking at the relation of the earth and the sun — one right and one wrong — so there are two ways of looking at the relation between a person and the daily events and routine cycle of life. Some people live in such a way as to have all their moods determined by what happens to them in the world. They are sad when stars take up their encampment on the battlefield of night; and they are cheerful in morning's eyes. When there is rain on the cheek of nature, often tears bedew their own cheeks. What happens at the bargain counter, in the office or in traffic; the poisoned arrow of sarcasm, the overheard slur and the whining of children, so often make and mold our moods, that like chameleons we take on the color of the experience that presently imposes itself on us. When we allow ourselves to revolve about circumstances, our feelings become like the seasons, shrinking when some hard service must be done and fainting in the face of every woe. Even love is reduced to fickleness so that the only love songs one hears now on radio and television are about "how happy we will be" when married; no longer does one hear the "silver threads among the gold," or the story of how happy the couple is that said they would be happy with "a girl for you, a boy for me." As Edna St. Vincent Millay expressed it in her poem, *I Know I Am But Summer*:

> I know I am but summer to your heart
> And not the full four seasons of the year.

The conditions of a happy life is to so live that the trials and vicissitudes of life do not impose their moods on us. Rather, we become so rooted in peace and inner joy that we communicate them not only to our surroundings, but also to others. Tennyson spoke of such a character "with power on thine own act and on the world." Some radiate cheer and happiness because they already have it within them, just as some seem to have ice on their foreheads, making winter all the year.

The problem is how to possess this inner constancy of peace which makes the depths of our soul calm, even when the surface, like the ocean, is ruffled or mixed with storms or cares. The best way is prayer which gives us independence of moods in two ways: first, it exhausts our bad moods, by telling them to God. The wrong way is to exhaust our bad feelings on human beings, because either they resent them, plan revenge, or they reciprocate by assuming an equally bad mood. Bringing them to God is exhausting them, just like bringing ice to the flame melts the ice. A very false theory in modern psychology is that whenever we feel pent up psychologically, we should give it a physiological outlet — for example, "forget it; go out and get drunk," or "when the passions are strong, satisfy them." If every son-in-law did this with a mother-in-law who was "moody" with him, the population of the country would be reduced by one-tenth. It is right to say that the mood must be emptied, but to empty it on ourselves, or on our fellow man, is to get it back either with a hangover or an enslaved condition we cannot break.

The second advantage of prayer is not only to void our bad moods, but to replace them with good feelings. As we pray, the sense of God's presence and law becomes more intimate; instead of wanting to "get even with our enemy," we take on God's attitude toward them, which is loving forgiveness and mercy. We may even reach a point, if we pray enough, where we become unsatisfied until we render good for evil. Gradually we see that it is far sadder to be a wrongdoer than to be the wronged one; the injurer is much more to be pitied than the injured. Eventually we get rid of moods, cultivate a constancy which never retaliates, even as Stephen did, who after the example of Our Lord, forgave those who stoned him (Ac 7:60). In the strains of life, nothing is as soothing and as strengthening as the comforting power of prayer.

57. *"How Noble in Reason"*

Everyone coming into the world has one great light sealed upon him, which is reason, or the faculty of knowing the true and the right. Some have an additional light, which is that of faith. The latter are fortunate, inasmuch as they have the extra illumination for the problems of life. As the eye has not its own light, but needs the sun, so too the reason for its perfection needs the gift of faith. We have the same eyes at night as we have in the day, but we cannot see in darkness because we lack the additional light of the sun. The reason those with faith have a keener insight into values and a deeper moral sense is because they are blessed with a light others lack.

But here we are concerned solely with first light, or reason. In these days of propaganda, superstition, denial of intellect, the exaltation of sentiment, and the domination of instinct, it is well to remind ourselves of our dignity, as Shakespeare did in saying: "What a piece of work is man! *How noble in reason! how* infinite in faculty!… in action how like an angel! in apprehension how like a god!" (*Hamlet*, Act II, Scene ii, Line 317).

Every person in the world is illumined with the light of reason, which is a reflection of the Divine Wisdom. We are like so many volumes issuing from the Divine Press. To each is given the freedom to write on those pages and thus do the autobiography of our character. Even though we write badly or well, indisputably stamped on the cover is the name of the Divine Author. Despite inkblots of moral value which are due to our moral carelessness, the Divine watermark is stamped on each page, untouched by our poor scribbling.

Reason manifests itself in different ways at different times. In the ancient world it was art that made civilization and culture; in our world it is science and technology. Art is the expression of beautiful ideals through the real. Michelangelo said that inside every block of marble is an admirable form; one need only hack away the nonessentials in order to reveal it. Science, however, is more concerned with law and order.

Every new invention, every newly discovered law, whether in biology, or astronomy, or physics, is in the truest sense of the word a "discovery." Columbus could not have discovered America if America were not "there." A scientist actually unwraps a secret, a rhythm, a melody, a law that God already placed in the universe. As Michelangelo "unwrapped" marble, so the scientist unwraps what has been hidden in the cosmos since the beginning.

Every scientist is a kind of proofreader. He is not the author of the law he enunciates. Few indeed are the great scientists who ever think so, even by confusing the carbon copy with the original. They know the difference between discovery and invention. Many have the vision of Wordsworth, who said that "the meanest flower that blows could give thoughts that often lie too deep for tears" (*Intimations of Mortality*, st. 11). But such thoughts are not given to those who do not think, and search for reason. The window lets in the light, but not to the blind.

The scientist of our modern civilization has a blessed advantage over most men, for to him is given a deeper vision of creation. One great scientist, Eddington, became so enamored of his findings in mathematical physics that he ended up his scientific treatise with a chapter on mysticism. This was going too far. But, at any rate, he did acknowledge, with Jeans, that all our scientific discoveries take us only to the edge of the picture. Then the philosopher must take over.

Blessed is the one to whom the universe is not opaque like a curtain, but transparent as is a window, and to whom reason's Author is seen behind every true act of reasoning.

As George Herbert expressed it:

> A man that looks on glass
> On it may stay his eye
> Or, if he pleaseth, through it pass
> And then the heavens espie.

58. Easter

Easter is the Feast of the Resurrection of Our Divine Lord from the grave, three days after He was crucified. On many occasions He had foretold: "No one takes My life from Me; on the contrary, I lay it down on My own" (Jn 10:18). On several occasions when there were attempted stonings, He told His enemies that it would do no good, for "My hour was not yet come" (Jn 2:4; 7:30; 8:20). It was not until Judas came into the Garden that He released the forces of evil and permitted them to do their worst: "The hour has arrived and the Son of Man will be handed over to sinners" (Mt 26:45). God has His day, but evil has its hour, and all that it can do is to turn out the Light of the world.

But what is most peculiar about Easter is that although His followers had heard Him say He would break the bonds of death, when He actually did, no one believed it. They had to be convinced beyond all shadow of a doubt. Of all the skeptics in the history of the world, none ever equalled the apostles and the disciples and the holy women. Voltaire and the like were credulous babes compared to them in skepticism. Contemporary attempts to explain away the belief in the Resurrection psychologically fail to take this doubt into account.

The followers were not expecting a Resurrection and, therefore, did not imagine they saw something of which they were ardently hoping. Even Mary Magdalene, who within that very week had been told about the Resurrection when she saw Lazarus raised to life from a grave, did not believe it. She came on Sunday morning to the tomb with spices to anoint a body — not to greet a Risen Savior. On the way, the question of the women was: "Who will roll us back the stone for us?" (Mk 16:3). Their problem was how they could get in; not whether the Savior would get out. When Magdalene found the grave empty, the Resurrection did not enter her mind. She ran to some of the disciples, saying, "They've taken the body from the tomb and we don't know where they've put Him" (Jn 20:2). Then she heard the rustling of someone in the bushes, she did not look up — so little was she anticipating seeing the Savior; she assumed that it was a gardener. Belief and expectancy are two factors that are absolutely essential for the production of psychological visions or imaginings, but both were lacking in the case of the disciples and the followers.

Finally convinced by vision, speech, and touch that He had risen, she now runs to Peter and John to tell them of the news. Their answer was an "explanation" of the supposed phenomenon, and a typical explanation it was for men. They said "it is a woman's tale; you know how women are; they are always imagining things — are credulous and superstitious." When finally they were convinced on empirical grounds, it took seven days of evidence to convince the rest of the apostles, one going so far as to demand the scientific test of putting his finger into the hands and his hand into the wounded side of Jesus, which evoked from the Savior the words: "Blessed are those who have not seen and yet have believed" (Jn 20:28).

A few years ago Frank Morison, a skeptic like the apostles, decided to write a kind of detective story on who stole the body, and thus gave rise to the "myth" of the Resurrection. His original venture, as he put it in his work, *Who Moved the Stone*, never came to port, but foundered on the rocks, and landed him on an "unexpected shore" — the belief in the Resurrection.

The Resurrection is the only answer to the question of the breach that we all feel psychologically in ourselves between the body and the soul.

Some thinkers through the ages sacrificed the body to the soul; today the tendency is to sacrifice the soul to the body. The Resurrection reveals the sacredness of both. No mere rational doctrine of immortality can do this perfectly. Furthermore, as for the Risen Lord, it lifts Him out of history and makes it possible for Him to enter into new relations with mankind. If He stayed with us in the flesh, He would have come no closer to us than the touch of a hand or an embrace. But ascending to the Father and sending His Spirit of Love into our hearts, He became not an example to be copied, or a fact to be remembered, but a life to be lived and a communion to be shared. Now it is possible for us to embrace the crosses and trials of this life, knowing that the "sufferings of this life simply cannot be compared to the glory that is to come" (Rm 8:18).

59. The Credulity of Unbelief

An age without faith is an age of superstition. Religious belief is so essential to the heart that once it is cast aside, some false form is called in to fill the void. Unless the house is tenanted with goodness, seven devils worse than the first come in to dwell there. When minds abandon their concern about final destiny, they substitute for the mystery of what happens after death, the mystery of how someone was murdered. But mystery there must be. At the end of the twentieth century we find ourselves living in an era of superstition in which minds believe everything as fanatics and quacks become shrines of worship and objects of adoration.

Whence came the millions to accept the superstition of Nazism, Fascism and Communism if it were not from an emptiness of soul brought about by a loss of faith? The essence of political superstition is the identification of the political and the sacred, as the essence of economic superstition is the Communist identification of the laboring class and Messianism. It was the great boast of the eighteenth century that "God" and "the supernatural" would be exorcized by an exposure to light. But what happened with the rejection of religious faith was the upsurge of political superstitions which came very close to making the world a madhouse. If there is not one great Face of Love that bends over mankind, its troubled mind will fill it with a thousand horrible masks. When religion is strong, it purges the unconscious mind of all those fears and anxieties, those worries and psychoses which psychoanalysis tries to expunge in the soul without faith. Even when psychoanalysis does effect what it calls a "transference" of the mental state, it never appeases the hunger of the soul for something spiritual and beyond self to adore and worship. Faith in a human being is not like sawdust in a doll. You cannot rip it open, shake out the sawdust on a couch, analyze its tree origins, put it back and make a new creature.

The thirsty traveler in the desert who mistakes a mirage for an oasis is superstitious. He has abandoned reason and sees a dream for a reality. So our twentieth century, impatient with its long voyage on the sea of life, after having denied a port and thrown away the compass, has turned clouds into islands and fog-banks into imaginary continents. Denying God, we seem to find it necessary to make gods, not out of gold and silver and clay, but out of science, psychology and economics.

Quite apart from the theology of it, the psychological fact stands out that those who have a deep and profound faith in Christ, the Son of God, are less likely to make unmanly submission to unworthy pretenders. This has been proven in thousands and thousands of cases in which Christian missionaries during times of persecution withstood their persecutors while those without faith succumbed. Freedom from dependence on "phonies" is purchased by loyalty to Truth and Love.

The grave danger of loss of faith is not only that others will arise to insist on dominating us, but that our wills will become so weak and our minds so confused as to insist on giving assent. Two women, after undergoing "brainwashing" in a political prison, were finally released. Both women returned to the relative freedom of their homes and families; in a few weeks they asked their captors to return them to prison because they wanted to be dominated. Superstition manifests itself not only in credulity, but also in servility. Scripture says the "last times" will be characterized by a refusal to endure sound teaching.

Many live under the illusion that their rejection of religious faith is a proof that they are immune from credulity. The truth is that they too accept authority, but it is the vague, vaporous, anonymous authority of "they." "They" are wearing green, and the like. Who are "they"? The person of faith at least knows the One Whose guidance he accepts. Few things are more strange than the eagerness with which many so-called educated people swallow the dicta of a mere human being, and swear by his glory. Great indeed is the void left in the heart by the exile of Christ.